May 15, 2010

Dear C

Happy Birthday!

I so enjoy our mutual love of baseball and find that our trips together to watch our favorite teams are always a joy. Looking forward to many more sojourns—

Love Dad

BATTING STANCE GUY

A Love Letter to Baseball

GAR
RYNESS

CALEB
DEWART

SCRIBNER
A Division of Simon & Schuster, Inc.
1230 Avenue of the Americas
New York, NY 10020

First Scribner trade paperback edition May 2010

SCRIBNER and design are registered trademarks of The Gale Group, Inc., used under license by Simon & Schuster, Inc., the publisher of this work.

For information about special discounts for bulk purchases, please contact Simon & Schuster Special Sales at 1-866-506-1949 or business@simonandschuster.com.

The Simon & Schuster Speakers Bureau can bring authors to your live event. For more information or to book an event, contact the Simon & Schuster Speakers Bureau at 1-866-248-3049 or visit our website at www.simonspeakers.com.

Design by Brian Chojnowski, illustrations by Natalie Long, and photographs by Caleb Dewart

WIFFLE,® WIFFLE® Ball, the image of the WIFFLE® ball are registered trademarks of The Wiffle Ball, Inc., of Shelton, CT, and used here with permission.

Topps baseball cards are used courtesy of The Topps Company, Inc.

Manufactured in the United States of America

1 3 5 7 9 10 8 6 4 2

Library of Congress Control Number: 2010005865

ISBN 978-1-4391-8113-3
ISBN 978-1-4391-8172-0 (ebook)

For

CAMERON, MAE,
LUCY & WILDER

CONTENTS

BEST OF THE REST

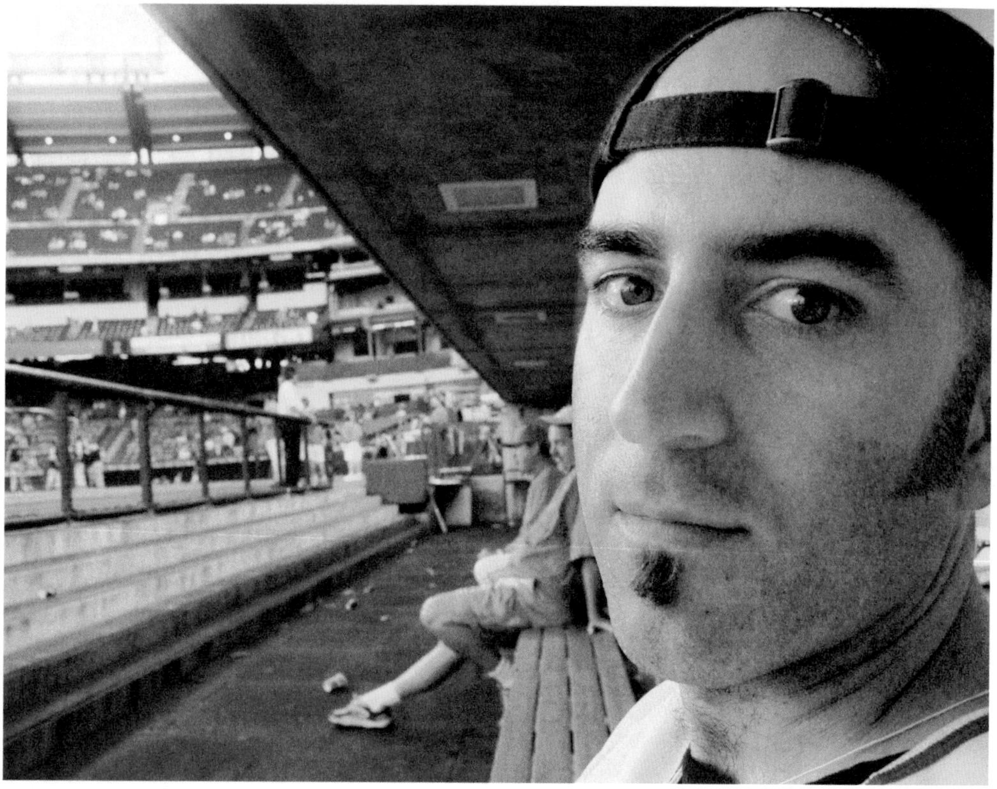

GAR RYNESS IS THE BATTING STANCE GUY.

And, if you ever meet him or watch him perform you'll understand that he's just a regular guy with an amazingly deep knowledge of baseball and a supremely odd and funny talent for mimicry. However, Gar did not create the Batting Stance Guy phenomenon alone. His co-conspirator, the guy who first turned on the video camera, is Caleb Dewart. Since posting the first video online, Gar and Caleb have worked together to share Batting Stance Guy and a love of baseball with the world. Even though this book contains Gar's stance imitations and his personal stories told first person, Gar and Caleb wrote the book together. With that said, now world powers can get back to solving the world's issues.

BATTING STANCE GUY

A Love Letter to Baseball

BATTING STANCE GUY

INTRODUCTION

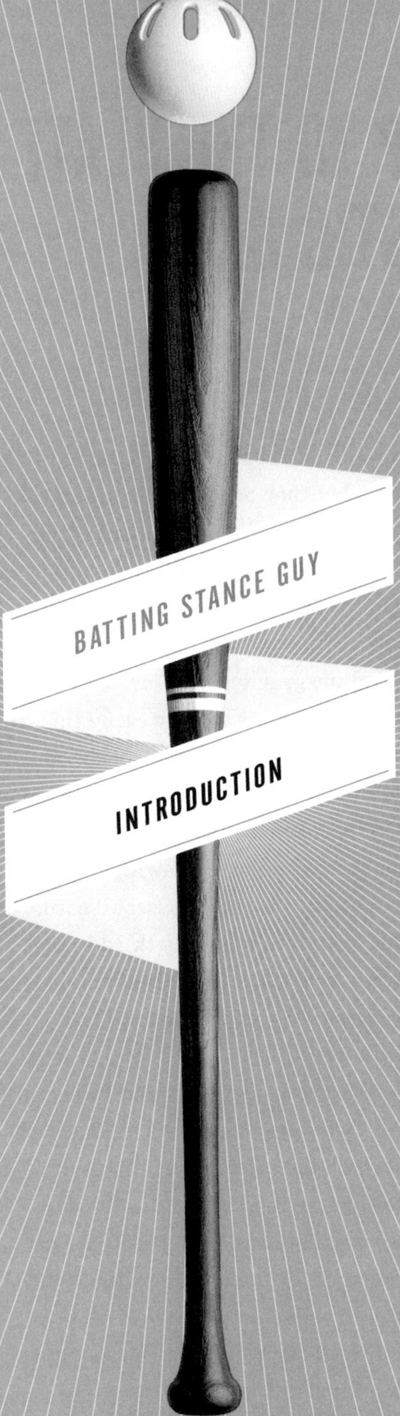

STEPPING UP TO THE PLATE... WITH A PLASTIC BAT

MY NAME IS GAR RYNESS AND I LOVE BASEBALL. I love my wife and children more, but they haven't been around as long as baseball, so there's a good chance that my memory of Sid Bream's slide in the 1992 NLCS and Dan Gladden's 1987 mullet are more vivid than the two things my wife just told me to remember at the grocery store.

But I never really understood the gravity of my love for the game until I started deconstructing my fan origins while writing this book. In first grade I repeatedly got in trouble with the teacher during coloring time because I was ruining all the green crayons. Each day I simply chose to draw a baseball field, leaving my classmates without any green to highlight their nonbaseball-related drawings. Every penny I earned from my paper route was spent on baseball cards. My second-grade Halloween costume was Pete Rose. My third-grade costume was Gary Carter. It's only now when I say these things aloud that it sounds strange. What Northern California kid went as a Montreal Expos catcher for Halloween? Ever?

We had a rule in our house. My brother, sisters, and I were only allowed to watch seven hours of TV a week. *This Week in Baseball* and NBC's *Game of the Week* took up the bulk of that time, with *The Cosby Show* and *Family Ties* taking the rest. When the TV was off, I'd take a random set of 25 baseball cards, go to the living room, draft a lineup, and fictitiously reenact an entire game with a Wiffle bat, glove, and my imagination. Daryl Boston would lead off in left field, Ken Landreaux in center field, Greg Walker at first base, Mike Schmidt at third base, Ken Singleton in right field, Dave Engle at catcher, Dickie Thon at shortstop, Jerry Royster at second base, then the pitcher. That lineup is insane, no rhyme or reason, not all

A
Halloween 1980. This answers the question about how long I've been imitating stances.

B
What eight-year-old in Northern California wasn't Gary Carter for Halloween in 1981?

C
For those of you wondering: my dad was not a Middle Eastern dictator.

A

expos

B

CUBS

C

PROPERTY OF
LOS ANGELES
Dodgers

NIKE

SOX

AL or NL, not heavy with players from a particular team, not a bunch of All-Stars. In fact, you might never have heard of some of them. Oh, here comes Al Cowens to pinch-hit for Jerry Augustine.

When I was 12 the most important thing in my life was taken away from me. I was a starting pitcher for our Little League 10- and 11-year-old All-Star team. It was a league that twice had teams play in Williamsport for the Little League World Series, so there's a chance that I had a promising future with limitless possibilities. Right around my twelfth birthday I felt a tremendous pain in my right shoulder. Ten months of tests revealed that I had a rare bone tumor the size of a golf ball in my right humerus—something that is not humorous at all. I was crushed to miss a quarter of seventh grade and have my right arm in a sling while on a crutch. They took bone out of my back to place in the shoulder where the tumor had eaten away the bone, so walking was difficult. The only bright side to the surgery was that my parents got my favorite player, Kent Hrbek, to wish me well with a letter that I should probably get framed someday. Most days some combo of Andy Gustafson, Kevin McCready, Mike Russello, and Todd Harlow would play stickball in my front yard. Not wanting to sit out, I began to pitch left-handed while my normal throwing right arm was in a sling. Senior League (13 to 15 years old) tryouts came two months after the surgery, and the doctors said it would be impossible for me to play right-handed. I didn't hesitate in my decision to play the entire season left-handed. Parents and coaches found my story heartwarming and courageous and fully supported my decision. Sadly, the ball didn't cooperate, lacking the courage to go where I aimed it. Though they were supportive, I'm also not sure my teammates found being on the receiving end of my throws very

Most kids pick one team, usually their home team, to follow. As you can see, I had a rather confused baseball identity.

heartwarming. I got through the season but, in the cold, harsh reality of Little League, it wasn't very pretty. I wasn't exactly Jim Abbott.

My right arm healed enough for me to play the following year as a righty. I made the team all four years of high school as the last guy on the bench. Occasionally getting into a game, I was mostly there for comic relief and emotional support for a group of players who were much better than I was ever going to be.

When I went away to college, my baseball career ended, but, as a resident of Northern California attending Syracuse University, I started to take some cross-country road trips. Andy McHargue, a classmate from Oakland and a fellow baseball fan, joined me for these adventures. On those trips we saw 19 baseball games. I didn't know it at the time, but this was the beginning of my journey to see a game in every stadium.

No longer buying baseball cards or needing autographs, I began to interact with females and see the world. I learned quickly that wearing a Kent Hrbek jersey to college parties wasn't the best way to impress the ladies.

College was a blur of intramural softball, cold winters, and occasional class attendance. I think it's safe to say that anyone who knew me in college will be surprised to find out that I've become a published author.

Through all of these experiences, I've never stopped imitating baseball players' batting stances. It's generally been a silly party trick or just a way to enhance a Wiffle Ball game, but it's something I've never been able to shake. It's like riding a bike. With that said, as I've started thinking about all the details of my life, I've started to feel like Chazz Palminteri turning around in *The Usual Suspects* after

As a kid, I'm not sure there was anything better than getting an entire box of unopened Topps packs.

A

HUMM
BABY!
CHEVROLET ALL-STAR WORKOUT

B

Roger "Verbal" Kint has told him the incredible tale. Chazz sees all the evidence on the wall after Kint is gone and is stunned. It's strange to wake up one day in my mid-30s, married with two daughters, working for a nonprofit, balding, athletically past my prime, and realize that I am a completely insane baseball fan. It may sound crazy, but I really never knew until it was all laid out in front of me.

So here it is—my love letter to baseball laid out in front of you. If you're expecting this to be an almanac or something even remotely comprehensive, buy another book. I'm not a baseball expert or an authority with any kind of credentials other than my unfettered love of the game. I hope that this book sits somewhere on the shelf between a Bill James abstract and the ramblings of a madman. I hope it makes you laugh, but more important, I hope it makes you take a deeper look at the game I—and, most likely, you—love. Baseball, if nothing else, is a game full of details. Its wonderfully slow pace allows for the subtleties and nuances of its characteristics and moments to be magnified for everyone to see. But as with most things in life, we all need to be reminded occasionally where to look.

There are a lot of things to love about baseball, but it's the phenomenon of the stance that caught my attention. It's the celebration of the individual in a team sport, a quick show of personality and flash in a world that generally looks for conformity. It's about music and theater and jazz hands and obsession and consistency (or inconsistency). Other sports have quirky actions that players perform when all eyes are on them—free throws, putting routines, end zone dances, high sticking, soccer players feigning injury—but nothing matches what hitters in baseball do at the plate.

As humans, we often brush off what we see in front of us. We some-

A
My bedroom in 1988. An obsession with Micro League baseball and trading cards did not help me get a girlfriend.

B
If I'd known that Joe Carter's Donruss rookie card would be worth $8 25 years later I wouldn't have used it to make my bike sound like a motorcycle.

times forget to really absorb what's going on around us. Think of this book as a magnifying glass. A (hopefully) moderately humorous magnifying glass aimed directly at baseball and its cavalcade of personalities.

There are 50 players I've tried to honor in this book, so it's a very loose "greatest 50 stances of all time" list. I've limited the list to the most interesting hitters of my lifetime. If you're an older fan and you're upset that I didn't include Pete Gray in this book, tough nuggets—I had to stick with who I remember. But I've also left plenty of those guys off the list. You might scratch your head when you notice that there isn't a full chapter on Nomar Garciaparra but there is one for Tony Eusebio. I'm sorry. Nomar's pre-stance antics are fascinating, but his actual stance doesn't make the top 50.

Matt Diaz, Joe McEwing, Luis Gonzalez, George Brett, Reggie Smith, Milt May, Edgar Martinez, Mackey Sasser, Dave Chalk, Mark Parent, Chris Stynes, Eugenio Velez, Doug DeCinces, Geoff Jenkins, Carl Yastrzemski, Nick Swisher, David Eckstein, Jesse Barfield, Carl Crawford, Bruce Bochte, Gary Roenicke, Keith Hernandez, Richie Hebner, Mike Schmidt, Mel Hall, Ryan Zimmerman, Carlos Quentin, Darryl Strawberry, Jody Davis, Al Bumbry, Dick McAuliffe, Lonnie Smith, Gerald Perry, Bake McBride, Cecil Cooper, and Cesar Cedeno are all players who didn't quite make the cut. And that's just to name a few. The best thing about baseball is that almost every hitter has his moment. Whether it's the flip of the bat and a rookie's excited run to first on a walk-off homer or the over-the-top reaction of a utility player to a brush-back pitch, there are moments of individual absurdity that happen every day in baseball.

Just don't forget to look.

A
The last time the Expos were good.

B
If I send this picture to the Pirates, I like my chances for a September call-up.

C
These are the forearms of a major league utility infielder. I took this picture of Chris Speier right before he threw me and his son Justin batting practice at Wrigley. Oddly enough, Justin played for the Angels more than 20 years later with Gary Matthews Jr., the son of "The Sarge."

A

PIRATES
14

B

I Know The
SARGE

C

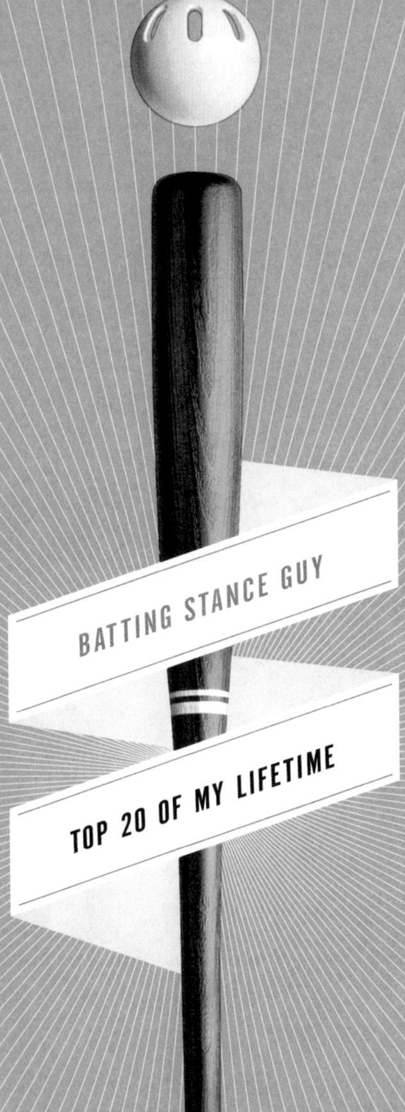
BATTING STANCE GUY
TOP 20 OF MY LIFETIME

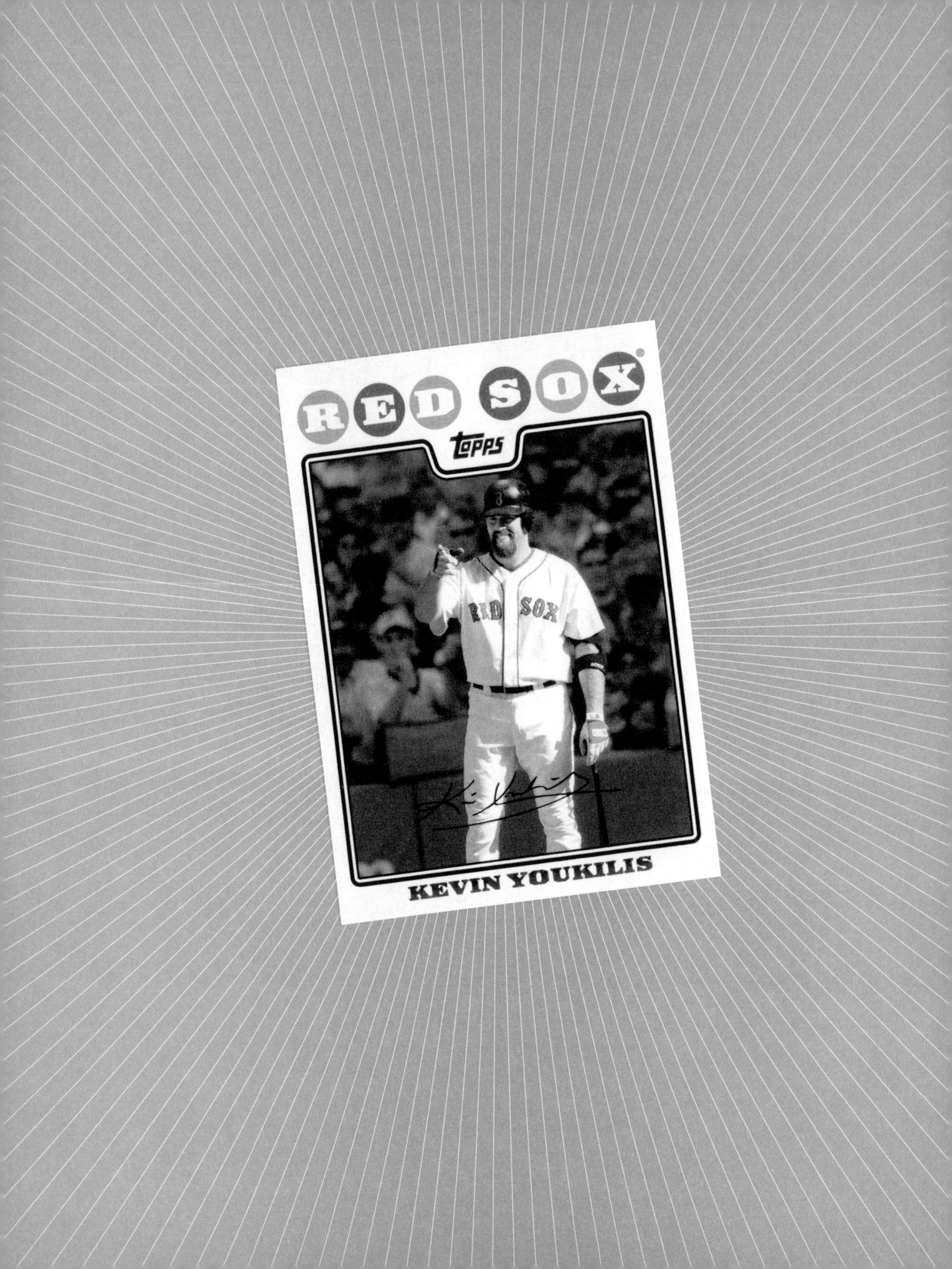
RED SOX
topps
RED SOX
KEVIN YOUKILIS

KEVIN YOUKILIS

KEVIN YOUKILIS IS MANY THINGS TO MANY PEOPLE. TO RED SOX FANS HE IS THE PRESENT AND THE FUTURE—A GUY WHO TOOK LESS MONEY THAN HE COULD HAVE TO STAY WITH THE SOX AND BECOME A LINCHPIN OF RED SOX NATION FOR YEARS TO COME.

To Yankees, Indians, Angels, and Rockies fans he's a no-good son of a %##$% whose patience at the plate and overcompetitiveness knocked them out of the postseason the past few years. To the facial hair club of North America (founding members include Scott Ian from Anthrax and the dudes in ZZ Top) he's not only the president but also a client. To Patrick Ewing he is the only man in American sports who sweats more than he does. And to Little League coaches all over the world he is the embodiment of what not to teach.

To me he is everything. If the batting stance is art, then he's Michelangelo. If the stance is a mountain, he's Everest, Kilimanjaro, and Mount Rushmore rolled into one. He's Tony Batista and Craig Counsell with better stats, playing on a team that people either love or hate. He's a perennial All-Star and MVP candidate with what is the most amazingly absurd batting stance in baseball history. He just makes baseball fun.

I had a chance to meet him in spring training, and I told him that while he has nothing riding on me, I have everything riding on him. I need him and players like him to succeed. There isn't a more requested player on the planet than Youkilis. From Dave Letterman and Jim Gaffigan to David Ortiz and Manny Ramirez, players and fans alike demand that I imitate him and roll over laughing when I do.

My question is this: How does a player like this have such insane stance antics and yet continue to be a top MVP candidate? It really defies logic, physics, and the common sense that every hitting coach in baseball, from Little League to the majors, must have.

It really just doesn't seem possible that Youkilis could hit the ball with so many moving parts to his stance. What's fascinating is that he really isn't aware of everything he does. He's like that really pretty girl in high school who just has no idea about what she's got going on.

Youkilis reminds me of an old Dave Valle quote. As a backup catcher for the Mariners, Dave was once asked about a young Ken Griffey Jr.'s swing. The Seattle backup catcher declared, "It's easy to hit over .300 with Griffey's swing. Try doing it with mine."

% A FEW VARIABLES IN YOUK'S STANCE

Try a few at-bats playing Wiffle Ball in your backyard with Youk's stance. Trust me, it will get you nowhere. Seriously—try it. Here's what you need to do:

1. Spread you hands about a mile apart on the bat.
2. Don't actually hold the bat with your right hand but instead move your right hand up and down the bat like you're petting a cat.
3. Hold the bat above your head and aim the head of the bat at the pitcher like Julio Franco used to do.
4. Shimmy and bounce like you're on *Dancing with the Stars*.
5. Keep your feet together like you're standing on top of a telephone pole.
6. Run a garden hose up your back and duct tape it to the top of your head. Turn the hose on so water runs down your face and off the tip of your nose.
7. Staple a ferret to your chin.

If you can do all that and even make contact with your mom's best stuff, I'd be shocked. How about doing all that and trying to hit Justin Verlander's 100-mile-an-hour fastball or Tim Lincecum's curveball? Impossible.

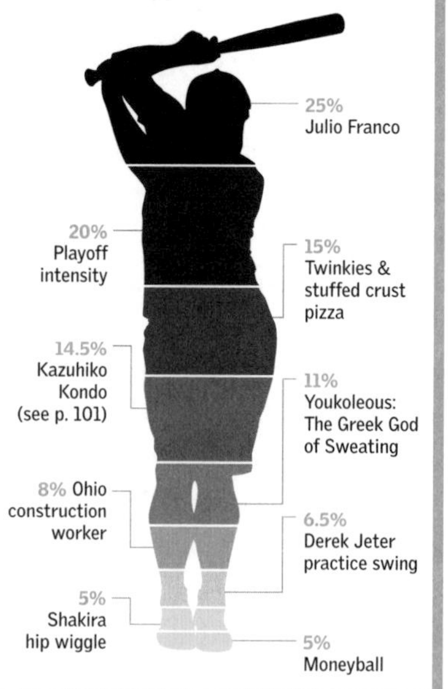

25% Julio Franco
20% Playoff intensity
15% Twinkies & stuffed crust pizza
14.5% Kazuhiko Kondo (see p. 101)
11% Youkoleous: The Greek God of Sweating
8% Ohio construction worker
6.5% Derek Jeter practice swing
5% Shakira hip wiggle
5% Moneyball

110% Youkilis

THE PRACTICE SWING

It's a great practice swing if you're chopping wood, which is why it looks nothing like his actual swing
He told me that he saw Jeter do this swing and he liked it

THE SETUP

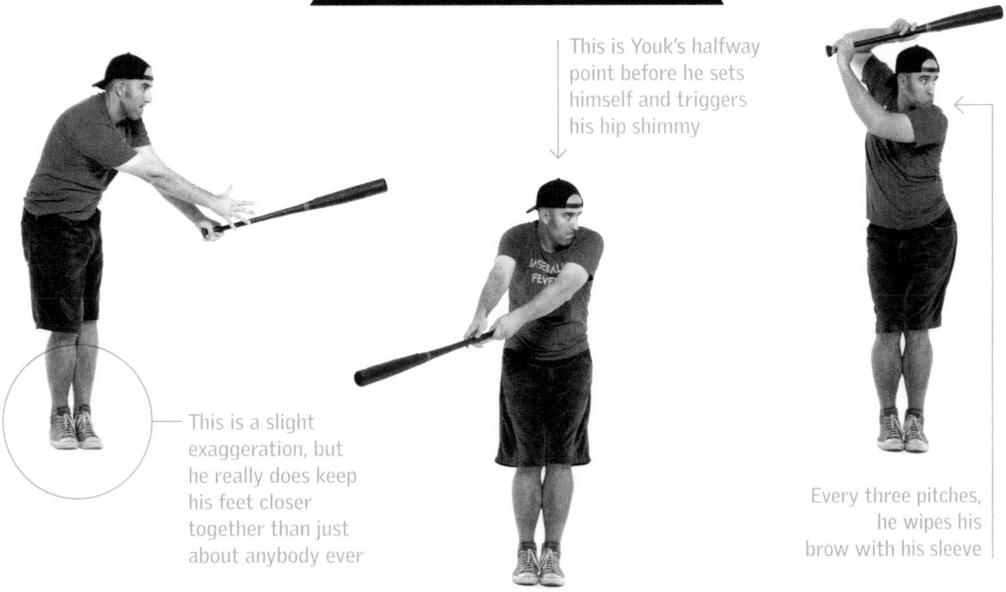
This is Youk's halfway point before he sets himself and triggers his hip shimmy
This is a slight exaggeration, but he really does keep his feet closer together than just about anybody ever
Every three pitches, he wipes his brow with his sleeve

THE SETUP (FRONT VIEW)

This is almost a hidden bat trick
Hip shimmy (cue the salsa music)

THE FOLLOW-THROUGH

If this looks strange, it should. Robb Quinlan is the only other guy I know who released the bat with the wrong hand

MY THOUGHTS ABOUT

THE BOSTON RED SOX and FENWAY PARK

In 1986 I lived on the West Coast with zero affiliation to either the Mets or the Red Sox. I liked Gary Carter from his Expos days and was pretty familiar with the Sox from watching *This Week in Baseball* and the NBC *Game of the Week*. When the Red Sox lost game six of the World Series the way they did I was stunned and sadder than usual, which didn't really make any sense. I wasn't rooting for either team, so why did I feel that way? It got weirder after game seven, when I left the living room and wept in my room. Baseball had really won me over. A week prior I couldn't have told you what team I was rooting for, but somehow the heartbreak and tragedy of that moment hit me like a ton of bricks.

Growing up, I didn't think of Boston as a crazy baseball town. I'm sure that sounds silly now, but as a kid my brain couldn't fathom that in the early '80s, with the Celtics and the Lakers in such high gear, it was possible that fans could care for more than one sports team at the same time. I always saw the packed crowds at Boston Garden and thought that Boston fans really loved their basketball. It wasn't until I went to college in Syracuse and met folks from places like Beverly and Canton and Revere and Swampscott that I started to get it.

It is fanhood to the deepest. I can make arguments for the best fans being Cardinal, Yankee, or Cub fans, but Red Sox fans are different. Joined by 86 years of futility, Red Sox fans had, until 2004, blind hope. The Yanks' and Cardinals' hope was based on something real. They'd won before and knew they'd be back. The Cubs' hope was and is funny and campy, but they revel in it. They're more interested in having a good time and taking in the good vibes of a Wrigley Field day game than obsessing about winning the big one. The Red Sox hope was crazy. It defied logic. Many self-respecting, law-abiding citizens with college degrees and the ability to converse on a variety of topics would blindly be let down and surprised when someone would eliminate the Sox. Didn't you know the Sox never had a chance?

No town has such strong feelings about average players. Bucky Dent and Aaron Boone had nice, polite careers, but are more discussed in Boston than in any city where they actually played. Those names elicit venomous anger, just as Bill Mueller and Dave Roberts will make any Sox fan smile. Sure, Boston fans have their radars locked on the big stars, but the little guys count just as much. What's hilarious about Boston fans is their loyalty to the uniform. It doesn't matter that Roger Clemens or Johnny Damon helped previous Sox teams win. They are absolutely dead to any self-respecting Sox fan. Their endlessly sarcastic chants of "Roger, Roger" in the 1999 ALCS were merciless. When Roger gave up five runs in two innings and got pulled from the game, Fenway went crazy.

Obviously, the recent success of the Sox makes it a whole lot harder for the average baseball fan to have much sympathy for Boston fans. Boston sports teams have rewarded their fans with an embarrassment of riches in the past few years. Heck, even the soccer team, the Revolution, is good. It's kind of silly. Luckily, the Yankees will always be the evil empire, collecting the best players like a mismatched game of Monopoly with your older brother. So the Sox, even as they spend and collect almost as wildly, will always play the role of underdog.

It's not even really worth writing anything about Fenway Park. Everyone knows it's one of the best venues in all of sports. The history, the feeling, the intimacy, and the setting are all phenomenal. With the exception of some obstructed views behind pillars, it's a magical place. Stand outside Fenway on Lansdowne Street during a game and you can just feel the electricity in the air. Hear a few people drop their r's and talk about Nomah sucking wicked bad after he left tha Sawx and you know you're in baseball heaven.

I saw David Wells and Roger Clemens pitch against each other at Fenway in April 1992. The weather was awful, amazingly cold and windy for spring. I was with eight buddies on Easter break from Syracuse. During the first rain delay we were talking about how crazy it would be to go on the field. After he'd heard enough, my buddy Ric Haupt quietly got up and walked onto the outfield grass while staring at us. Hilarious. Then one by one we hopped on the field to take pictures. Ric Haupt taught me a very important life lesson: It's easier to ask forgiveness than permission.

Boston, Massachusetts / Fenway Park: April 17, 1992: the day I discovered Fenway Park security's blind spot. I'm not quite sure how I didn't get arrested walking on the field and posing for this picture before Roger Clemens beat Toronto's David Wells, 1–0.

DIAMONDBACKS™
Topps
ARIZONA
Craig COUNSELL
THIRD BASE
4

CRAIG COUNSELL

I WAS INVOLVED WITH A FEATURE THAT AIRED ON ESPN CALLED "ART OF THE STANCE."

They got a bunch of players including Cal Ripken, Youkilis, and Julio Franco to talk about their stances, and they intercut footage of various hitters with me imitating them. The producer of the segment told me that Craig Counsell was the lone conscientious objector. "He doesn't do that stance anymore," his people told ESPN. Wow. I could rattle off about 50 absurd pop culture analogies that give context to what a statement like that is like. It's an old story, really. It's the story of a man haunted by his past. A man perhaps embarrassed and ashamed of the things he did in his youth. Or it's the story of a true artist who doesn't need to play his old stuff in concert for his fans even though nobody is buying the new record.

Comedian was a vaguely interesting documentary that came out in 2002 about Jerry Seinfeld preparing for a new HBO stand-up comedy special. What made the documentary watchable was that it followed Jerry as he did something few comics have ever done: he threw out his entire stand-up act. This is a really big deal. What you learn watching this movie, and what you notice if you've ever seen a comic do his or her act more than once, is that successful stand-up is about telling the same jokes over and over and over again. People told Jerry he was nuts for throwing out his whole act, one he'd spent years perfecting before he got a television show and made enough money never to have to work again.

What's most interesting about Counsell is that he's done just what Jerry did, but repeatedly. He's completely changed his stance every time he's gone to a new team. Out with the old and in with the new. And we're not talking minor changes. Ripken's adjustments over the years were constant and generally subtle, the violin being the one really absurd standout. Counsell made radical adjustments.

Counsell may have denied ESPN, but he was all smiles in the Brewers' stretching circle when I had a chance to perform some imitation fun for the team during a weekend series in Milwaukee.

For those of you who quit sports before high school, the locker room can be a brutal place, and not just because it smells like feet and sour milk. It's like a Comedy Central roast. Teammates are merciless, nothing is off-limits, and you're naked half the time. You've got to have remarkably thick skin.

With Prince Fielder and Mike Cameron as ringleaders and every player a target, my afternoon with the Brewers was a classic ordeal of locker room hilarity. And Counsell was game. His smile went wide, and he squinted his eyes just like he does when he's at bat. He was a great sport, and the entire Brewers roster laughed when I asked him if he ever considered coiling his head all the way around when he was with the Diamondbacks, like Linda Blair in *The Exorcist.* I chronicled his Indians-era Jim Thome-esque stance with the Marlins, where the bat was right in front of his face, as well as his early Brewers stance, which was absolutely spectacular. In recent years, he's been subdued, but a few years ago he was raising his bat higher than anyone else in baseball history. For real. In a book full of superlatives, I tell you to ignore anything else ridiculous and grandiose that I've said and just firmly believe this one thing: nobody has reached higher with his bat than Counsell.

Thing is, that only *might* be Counsell's most amazing baseball feat, because he has two others to his credit. Did you know that there have been only two times in Major League Baseball history when a team has entered the bottom of the ninth inning of the seventh game of the World Series with the lead and lost the World Series and that Counsell played in both games? Against Jose Mesa and the Cleveland Indians in 1997, Counsell hit an RBI sac fly to right to tie the game and send it to extras. Two innings later, he scored the winning run on Edgar Renteria's single off Charles Nagy.

Fantastically, in 2001, Counsell was plunked by Mariano Rivera in the ninth inning to load the bases one batter before Luis Gonzalez singled in Jay Bell for the Diamondbacks' lone title. Incredible.

It really is possible that Counsell is the Forrest Gump of Major League Baseball. I mean that as a compliment, by the way. He's done it all, done it in his own way and been involved in some pretty amazing moments in baseball history. He should have a special place in Cooperstown next to Mark Lemke, Gene Tenace, and Brian Doyle. Not unlike the bat Counsell held, he rose to the greatest heights when the most people were watching.

COUNSELL'S BATTING AVERAGE FOR EACH STANCE
.300
.250
.200
BATTING AVERAGE
WACKINESS OF STANCE
He won a ring with this stance
.253 MARLINS
.218 DODGERS/ MARLINS
No wonder the '09 Brewers didn't make the playoffs— B.O.R.I.N.G.
.285 '09 BREWERS
.269 WITH DIAMONDBACKS
He won another ring with this stance
Bending your knees only makes this look slightly less crazy
.402 2012 NIPPON HAM FIGHTERS
Special SUGGESTED STANCE
.241 '04 BREWERS
I think Casey Kasem said it best when he said: "Keep your feet on the ground and keep reaching for the stars"

Let's see: greatest closer in postseason history versus scrawniest hitter to ever hit 57 home runs. How will this end? No way it ends on a bloop single to center.

Looks like another broken bat. Let's hope Torre didn't bring the infield in.

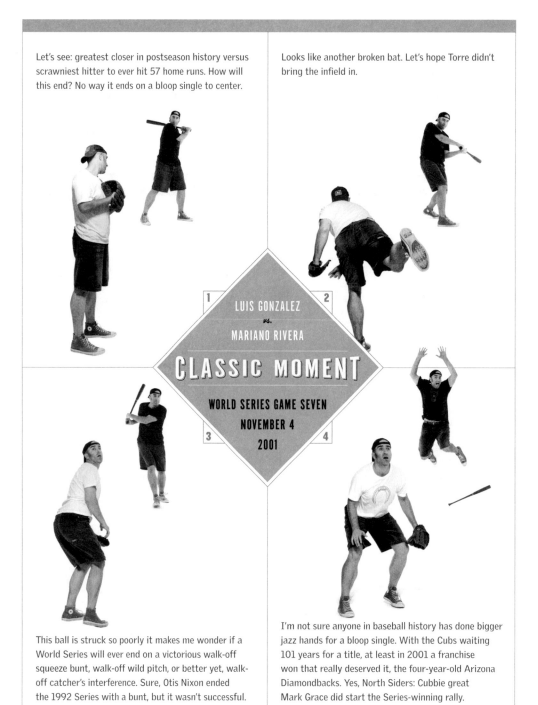

1 2 3 4

LUIS GONZALEZ

vs.

MARIANO RIVERA

CLASSIC MOMENT

WORLD SERIES GAME SEVEN

NOVEMBER 4

2001

This ball is struck so poorly it makes me wonder if a World Series will ever end on a victorious walk-off squeeze bunt, walk-off wild pitch, or better yet, walk-off catcher's interference. Sure, Otis Nixon ended the 1992 Series with a bunt, but it wasn't successful.

I'm not sure anyone in baseball history has done bigger jazz hands for a bloop single. With the Cubs waiting 101 years for a title, at least in 2001 a franchise won that really deserved it, the four-year-old Arizona Diamondbacks. Yes, North Siders: Cubbie great Mark Grace did start the Series-winning rally.

MY THOUGHTS ABOUT

THE ARIZONA DIAMONDBACKS and CHASE FIELD

The swimming pool just over the right-field fence at Chase Field in Arizona takes me back to my youth. The kids in my neighborhood played stickball with a tennis ball, a Little League Easton Big Barrel bat, and our garage door as the backstop. A home run was over Mike Russello's fence. A mind-blowing, out-of-the-park-like-Cecil-Fielder-in-Detroit home run was known as a "pooler," which entailed launching one cleanly into the Russellos' backyard and into the pool.

The similarities between my childhood games and Chase Field might end there, because when we retrieved the ball from the Russellos' pool there were rarely any half-drunk investment bankers spilling beer on their girlfriends with lower-back tattoos nearby.

With that said, the pool at Chase Field leads me to believe that the Diamondbacks might use ghost runners at some point. Also, if the Diamondbacks decide not to use a catcher, a "knobber" is a perfect strike, and if a player on the field swears loudly, someone's dad will quickly march out onto the field and address them like this: "Buster, what did you just say?"

The D-Backs beat the Yankees in the 2001 World Series, putting a crown on an incredible start for an expansion team. They were the fastest expansion team to make the playoffs (they did it two years in) and the fastest to win it all (four years in). The Marlins and the Rockies also have enjoyed almost instant gratification, which says a lot about what free agency, loads of money, and some good fortune can bring to any franchise that isn't the Rangers, Mariners, or Padres.

The 2001 D-Backs' roster was a who's who of solid veterans who had great careers with other teams. Matt Williams, Mark Grace, Curt Schilling, Randy Johnson, Tony Womack, Reggie Sanders, and Steve Finley were all guys looking for a last stop. Any one of them could have ended up like Wade Boggs on the Rays, playing out his last days on a basement-dwelling team in a city with virtually no fans. Okay, it wasn't the last stop for Schilling or Johnson, but it should have been for Johnson, whose inability to retire can only be compared to Jerry Rice.

The 2001 Yankees were winning game seven in the bottom of the ninth inning with a closer who had never blown a World Series save. They'd also won four of the previous five World Series and seemed destined to steamroll a team that really seemed to have no business being there. Gonzo lofts a single over Derek Jeter's head, Jay Bell scores, and the rest is history that will be written about in Curt Schilling's autobiography, tentatively titled *Was It Something I Said?*

Phoenix, Arizona / Chase Field:
This game in May 2000 ended when Damian Miller hit a grand slam off Orel Hershiser in the bottom of the 12th inning to win it for the D-Backs.

Topps HERITAGE
BLUEJAYS
TONY BATISTA
Tony Batista

TONY BATISTA

TONY BATISTA'S LOT IN LIFE, MUCH LIKE MOISES ALOU, WAS HAVING A HANDFUL OF LESS THAN BELOVED TEAMS AS EMPLOYERS. BATISTA SPENT TIME WITH THE BLUE JAYS, EXPOS, ORIOLES, DIAMONDBACKS, AND NATIONALS DURING HIS 11-YEAR BIG LEAGUE CAREER.

He hit a career-high 41 home runs in 2000 for a Toronto team that finished third in the American League East. He hit 32 homers for the 2004 Expos, who finished dead last in the National League East. If a bear hits homers in the woods, does anyone notice?

Thanks to all that, Batista is also in the dubious group of players, including current hitters—Randy Winn, Mike Sweeney, and Michael Young—who have played a ton of games without ever making the playoffs. Of Batista's 1,309 games, not a single one had the smell of playoff intensity, unless you count Batista's last game in the majors in 2007, when he pinch-hit for the Nationals in the final game of the regular season, against the Phillies. Jamie Moyer pitched five scoreless innings for the Phillies and Ryan Howard hit his 47th home run of the season in the Phillies' 6–1 victory. The Phillies won the East, one game ahead of the Mets, who were eliminated from the wild-card race in a loss to the Marlins, while the Nationals finished fourth, two games up on the Marlins, who finished last. Yeah, that probably shouldn't be counted.

One of the few times I've ever seen Gary Sheffield smile was in a *This Week in Baseball*–style piece about batting stances. He was asked who has the craziest stance he'd ever seen and he laughed and smiled and said, "Oh, Batista." He may have even been shaking his head. Batista played for the Fukuoka SoftBank Hawks in 2005, and you understand why when you see how he batted. His stance is classic Japanese—dead-pan comedy with an almost unparalleled flair. I'm sure the Fukuoka scouts saw a tape of Batista and decided they had to have him.

At the plate, Batista faced the pitcher, sticking both hands out toward the pitcher like a double-fisted version of Ichiro's samurai pose, looking through the bat at his opponent. The only other time I've seen that pose was in line at the midnight screening of *Star Wars: Episode 1* in May 1999. The only real difference is that Batista was a lot more athletic than any of my peers dressed in Jedi robes.

After his fighter pose, Batista would square his shoulders up while keeping his stance completely open from the waist down. As the pitch was delivered, he massively shifted his weight, swinging his left leg around while keeping it almost completely straight. I've got a less than elementary understanding of math, science, and theories of rela-whatever, but all this twisting and contortion has me highly confident that Batista truly defied basic laws of physics with his stance. Maybe he was more like a Jedi than I thought. There's at least a 25 percent chance that the Force was involved.

TWO-HANDED SAMURAI POSE

This isn't a side view. He's facing the pitcher

Feet still
haven't moved,
which is weird
Knees aren't
bent, which
starts to hurt
← I showed →
my chiropractor
these pictures
when he asked
me how I
threw my back out
I love the
high strike
Bends the
knees for the
first time
The finish of
the swing is
the only
normal thing
about Batista

CLASSIC MOMENT

MITCH WILLIAMS

vs.

JOE CARTER

WORLD SERIES GAME SIX

OCTOBER 23

1993

1

As a middle-aged man with virtually no hair, I'm not sure what I'm more jealous of at this moment: Mitch's outstanding mullet or Joe's Kid 'n Play high-top fade.

2

Mitch told me that he couldn't wait to pitch to the on-deck hitter: Darnell Coles. He quickly added that he never got the chance. Oops.

3

I'm a youth baseball coach and I have yet to find a pitching video that teaches pitchers to fall down and to brace themselves with their glove arm. I think I broke my wrist in this picture.

4

I'm pretty sure Mitch wishes he could have that pitch back. It was his last pitch as a Phillie.

MY THOUGHTS ABOUT

THE TORONTO BLUE JAYS and ROGERS CENTRE

The Blue Jays really do have their work cut out for them. Say what you want about cellar-dwelling teams like the Pirates and Reds, at least they have fans who grew up with an awareness of baseball as a game that's actually played. Baseball is a distant fourth to hockey, softball, and curling in Canada, which makes for a unique brand of baseball fan in Toronto. Add being in the American League East, with the Red Sox and the Yankees, to the equation, and you've got a tough baseball road for the Blue Jays. My first visit to SkyDome (now Rogers Centre) in Toronto was the first time I'd ever experienced fans cheering louder for the visiting team than for the home team. It was 2003 and the Red Sox were in town with the Boston road show, which explains why Roy Halladay was being heckled.

Rogers Centre aka SkyDome was built right before the retro-park renaissance, so it's got that giant, AstroTurfed, multiuse vibe that just wouldn't fly in the States anymore. It screams late '80s despite having a retractable roof and a hotel in it. I will say that the best view of any hotel room in the world is the Marriott inside the dome. A few years ago I spent one magical night in a room there that looked out over the field. Watching a game from my room was incredible, as was sleeping next to an empty ball field. It made me want to open my window, rappel down the side of the hotel wall, and run onto the field in the middle of the night. Waking up the next morning to see a bunch of overweight construction workers taking softball batting practice wasn't so magical.

The best perk of my quasi-fame are the multiple phone conversations I've had with Lloyd Moseby, a player who no doubt takes the title for most bizarre Blue Jays play in team history. In old Exhibition Stadium in Toronto, Moseby stole second base, only to get confused by a radically errant catcher's throw that went way over the second baseman's head and into center field. Moseby, thinking the ball had been caught on a fly ball out, retreated to first base. The center fielder hesitated and threw back to first base. The ball hit Moseby as he slid back into first base and got past the first baseman. Moseby then got up and ran safely to second base. He grabbed his helmet with both hands once he realized what had occurred.

Moseby stole 37 bases and hit 18 home runs for the 1985 Blue Jays, a team that was arguably done in by poor timing and rule changes. That was the first season the League Championship Series went to a best-of-seven series from a best-of-five. The Blue Jays rushed out to a 3–1 lead in the series on the Royals, only to lose the AL pennant in seven games. Every year prior, they would have ended up in the World Series after winning three games in the series.

It's not all grim history for the Blue Jays. They won back-to-back World Championships in 1992 and 1993, and despite not making the postseason since, have been pretty competitive in an obviously very tough division. Roy Halladay, Aaron Hill, Alex Rios, and Vernon Wells all came up with the team, a testament to a solid organization that scouts well. The fact that Halladay is now a Phillie is not the organization's fault. How can you fight the economic realities of a country that'd rather watch fight highlights from a Camrose Kodiaks and Salmon Arm Silverbacks game than see a baseball game?

Toronto, Ontario, Canada / Rogers Centre (formerly known as SkyDome):
This is my daughter eating fries at the best Hard Rock Café location in the world.

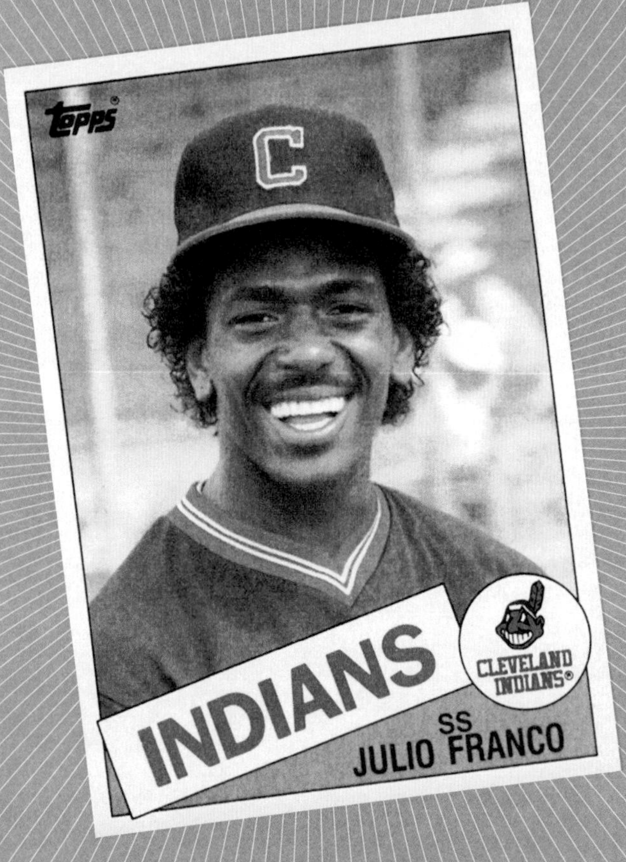
Topps
INDIANS
CLEVELAND INDIANS
SS
JULIO FRANCO

JULIO FRANCO

JULIO FRANCO REALLY WAS AN AGELESS WONDER. LIKE RICKEY HENDERSON, HE PLAYED BALL WELL INTO HIS MID-60S. HE JUST COULDN'T GIVE IT UP. HE WAS THE OLDEST PLAYER IN MAJOR LEAGUE BASEBALL HISTORY TO HIT A HOME RUN AS WELL AS THE OLDEST TO HIT A GRAND SLAM.

A model of consistency, he had the same stance at 40 that he had at 19. In fact, he says he was hitting like this when he came out of his mother's womb. He's the case study for what Cal Ripken was not. They both enjoyed nice careers and both hit well. But Franco definitely enjoyed a fuller head of hair. And unlike Cal, he picked the wackiest stance possible and stuck with it through thick and thin.

Kevin Youkilis owes him a debt of gratitude. As Youk dreamed of a major league career in his crib as an infant, Franco was pounding out hits with one of the most iconically odd stances of all time. Right before Billy Beane thought about him, Youkilis bought that McMansion of a stance from Franco and turned it into a castle, building several gaudy additions. The neighbors may not have been very happy, but Youk's value skyrocketed.

What was that stance? What was he really trying to do? The head of the bat pointing at the pitcher, the knees knocked together, and the back foot moving on his follow-through. If you ask any casual baseball fan who grew up in the '80s, they'll remember Julio Franco's stance. They may not remember

Youkilis is from Ohio, Franco played for the Indians in the '80s... it's starting to make sense

anything else about him, but they'll remember that. And they remember it because it made no sense. Franco made the Rangers and the Indians interesting for a lot of fans during some very lean years.

I've been told that Franco is still in tremendous shape. He needed a heavy workout to continue holding his bat like that. There's a reason why gravity grounded Yaz and Carew: lack of exercise. Carew and Yaz played in the era before the weight room and nutrition were really part of the game. Franco was a star in the '80s, when everything changed. You know how at some charity event, Rich Gossage will meet Billy Wagner and the two will immediately have a conversation as if they've known each other for years? You'll see the same thing when Britney Spears hugs Pamela Anderson, and they'll connect as old friends even though it's the first time they've met. It's about the unspoken bond they have and the shorthand of life experience that draws them together.

Players who share wacky batting stances aren't like that at all. If you take Acting 101 in college, one of the first things you learn

This is really
Youkilis from
the knees up

is that no one thinks he or she is crazy. Meaning if you are playing a character in a scene who is crazy, that character may be behaving crazily but doesn't think he's crazy. Julio Franco and everyone else in this book are crazy, but they just don't know it. I'm pretty sure Julio Franco doesn't watch former San Francisco first baseman Damon Minor and think, "Wow, that poor kid has a crazy stance just like mine; I'm gonna go talk to him and take him under my wing." These players get so focused on what they're doing that they honestly don't realize how crazily they are behaving.

If we had a party at Julio Franco's Florida home and invited every player in this book, none of them would make the connection. They'd probably just wonder why they got invited to a party with a bunch of weirdos.

You're right, this looks like a hockey slap shot

MY THOUGHTS ABOUT

THE TAMPA BAY RAYS and TROPICANA FIELD

Teams are bad until they're not. So until 2008, I didn't think it was possible for the Rays to finish a season as high as third place in the AL East. Often, sports reporters root for the big turnaround. It's why Indians Joe Carter and Cory Snyder graced the cover of *Sports Illustrated* in April 1987. That same optimism was on display when *S.I.* featured Delmon Young and Elijah Dukes on a 2005 cover. Sadly, those two didn't exactly endear themselves to Rays fans or ownership, although Matt Garza and Jason Bartlett did arrive via the trade for Delmon Young. The Rays' turnaround was without forewarning. A payroll only slightly higher than my buddy's landscaping business, incredibly young players, a loose fan base, and a junky stadium didn't exactly telegraph success in 2008. But there they were in the World Series after breaking the hearts of Red Sox Nation.

The Red Sox and the Yankees are banking on Tampa Bay falling victim to the curse of all small-market teams, because if the Rays are either lucky or bold enough to keep their young free agents, then the American League East is in trouble. Two thousand nine was a letdown year, but they've got a bunch of young studs who probably will end up making eight figures for the Yankees in a few years. The Rays did lock up Evan Longoria for the foreseeable future, which is a great sign if you've retired to Tampa, or you're Hulk Hogan.

When doing the Rays' pregame show in 2009, I walked into the dugout to retrieve my hat, and I heard a voice behind me say, "Hey, Batting Stance Guy." I turned around, and it was Longoria. I told him that I had been in the Rockies' stretching circle the month before where I told Troy Tulowitzki that he did the "Longoria neck." Troy strongly objected, saying, "He does my neck! I was called up first." Longoria laughed heartily and agreed.

More baseballs strike catwalks, lights, and speakers in fair territory at Tropicana Field than anywhere else I can think of. Growing up, we had a tree that hung over fair territory in our stickball game, but this seems less charming. The Trop cost $130 million to build, so its dysfunction as a sports venue is a little absurd. Sure, Jerry Jones just built a $1 billion stadium and misfired with his huge plasma TV screen for the fans, but somehow that seems amazingly cool and not pathetic in quite the same way as the catwalks of the Trop. Jerry's TV is high-definition, you know. The Trop routinely gets pegged as one of the worst stadiums in baseball. I've been treated very well by Rays fans and Rays players so it's hard for me to hate it too much. On a recent trip to Tampa, the Rays staff allowed me to walk the famous catwalks along the roof. It was both frightening and exhilarating to imitate Evan Longoria from high above the field.

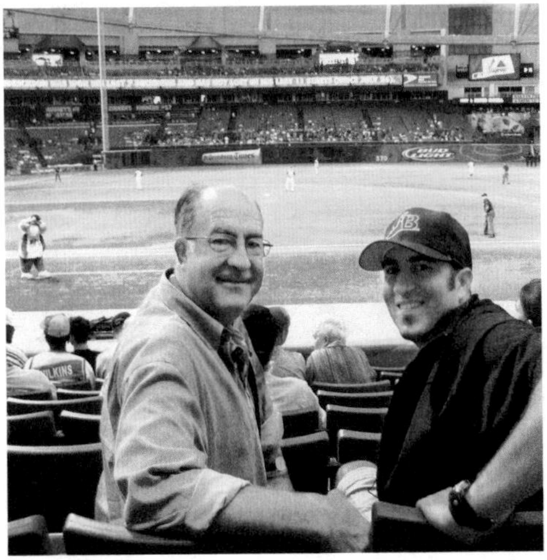

Tampa Bay, Florida / Tropicana Field:
I'm pretty sure that's a fan who just brought his own mascot outfit to the park and somehow got on the field.

topps
A'S
OUTFIELD
RICKEY HENDERSON

RICKEY HENDERSON

RICKEY BEING RICKEY. BORN IN THE BACK OF A CAR ON CHRISTMAS DAY, RICKEY WAS AND IS A TRUE ORIGINAL. SO MUSCULAR, SO FAST, SO EGOTISTICAL, SO ALOOF, AND SO MONEY, I'M PRETTY SURE HE THOUGHT HE HAD A LOT MORE IN COMMON WITH JESUS THAN THE REST OF US.

With such flair and pizzazz, he was made to play baseball. A "Rickey Rally" really was truly a self-made phenomenon. Rickey walks or singles, steals second base despite everyone in the stadium knowing that it's going to happen, goes to third base on a groundout, and strolls home on a sac fly. Nothing happened and he scored. It takes four doubles to score Big Papi from second, Bengie Molina gets thrown out on singles to left, and sometimes Matt Stairs doesn't score on a home run.

But Rickey wasn't just fast. Rickey was incredibly stylish. He would finish his swing with a split-second delay, holding the bat out front and then dropping it, realizing full well that he could take as much time as he wanted to get to first because nobody was going to catch him. On one of his many leadoff home runs, he would take a strange sidestepping angle to first base while popping his collar. Incredible. In 1991 I went to a Tuesday night game to see him break Lou Brock's all-time stolen-base record. Naturally, he did it the next day. Cutting school to see an A's day game seemed like a bad idea at the time. But now at 37, I sure wish I could've heard, "Today, I am the greatest of all time," live. That's just Rickey being Rickey.

Whether true or not, my favorite Rickey story involves his stint with the 1999 Mets, one of nine teams he played for during his 25-year career. Upon meeting new teammate John Olerud, he told him that he once played with another first baseman who also wore a batting helmet in the field. Olerud didn't have the heart to tell Rickey that they'd already been teammates on the Blue Jays. It reminds me of a baseball fan who called me some ugly names in the comments section of our Yankees YouTube video, telling us we're fake fans and that we could learn something from the guys who did the Red Sox stance video. Uh, that was us, too.

There isn't another Hall of Famer I can think of who ended his career with several years in the minor leagues. That is, unless José Offerman is in the Hall of Fame. Rickey just couldn't accept not playing baseball. I'm guessing that it was a case of him loving the game so much that he couldn't stand to be away from it and loving himself so much that he couldn't imagine the game without him. Has any player unretired after getting inducted into the Hall of Fame? If not, I'm pretty sure Rickey will be the first. Rickey was the best leadoff hitter of all time.

He changed the way games were managed. He changed the strike zone. He changed the way pitchers held runners on base. He was a 10-time All-Star and two-time World Series champion who did it all with the showmanship of a Vegas magician.

Putting your head in the strike zone feels dangerous

After he swung, he brought the bat all the way back and dropped it like a hot potato

So you think you can dance? Do this all the way to first base without getting thrown out and you'll be a Hall of Famer
← Pop that collar

MY THOUGHTS ABOUT

THE OAKLAND ATHLETICS *and* OAKLAND-ALAMEDA COUNTY COLISEUM

The Oakland A's of the '80s are fully to blame for my fascination with batting stances. When you attend any event as a kid and anyone is putting on a show like Rickey Henderson did at the plate, it will capture your imagination. Rickey was just the start. It continued when Carney Lansford came over in a trade and wiggled and gripped his bat, with Ron Hassey's dramatic bat waving, Dwayne Murphy swinging out of his shoes, Tony Phillips coiling into a knot, and Richie Hebner finishing his career in an unbelievable crouch. Throw in Jack Clark playing right field for the godawful early '80s Giants, and my future as Batting Stance Guy was cemented.

The Bash Brothers changed the complexion of Bay Area baseball. Tony LaRussa was managing, and home runs were flying out of the park. Pitching coach Dave Duncan picked Dave Stewart off the scrap heap of baseball and turned him into a four-time 20-game winner. That team just kept winning, but I no longer rooted for them because I'd fallen in love with the Minnesota Twins, who were in the same division. I attended one playoff game in 1988. It happened to be the lone World Series victory for the A's that year; one of only 15 World Series games to end in a walk-off home run. McGwire hit a bomb off Jay Howell. Amazingly enough, that Series featured two walk-off homers: McGwire's, and Kirk Gibson's pinch-hit homer that dramatically ended game one.

I've been to more A's games than any other team so I feel confident telling you that Oakland-Alameda County Coliseum is a below-average place to watch a baseball game. Unless something has changed that I don't know about, it's got the biggest foul territory in Major League Baseball, a claim to fame that no one should be proud of. Pretty soon it will be the last mixed-use stadium in Major League Baseball, and I'm not sure there's anything more desperate than the massive tarps they use to cover seats to make the capacity smaller. It's like putting a towel over an elephant and expecting everyone in the room to pretend they don't see him. What's the point exactly? Oakland was last in attendance in 2009.

Twins
14

Oakland, California / Oakland-Alameda County Coliseum: July 7, 1991: the first time I ever sneaked onto a major league baseball field. The A's were out of town, the back gate was open, and there was no security in sight. The terrorists really have won now that moments like this aren't possible anymore.

topps
GARY SHEFFIELD

GARY SHEFFIELD

THIS IS THE ONLY PERSON I NEED TO LIKE MY IMITATIONS. IF BRIAN GILES, KOSUKE FUKUDOME, YADIER MOLINA, OR TONY CLARK DON'T LIKE MY IMITATIONS THEN SO BE IT. SHEFFIELD IS DIFFERENT. THAT'S LIKE CARLOS ZAMBRANO NOT LIKING IT. IN FACT, PLEASE NO ONE SHOW SHEFF THIS BOOK. I CAN'T TAKE THE REJECTION.

I respect Sheffield's abilities, and I don't want to end up on his bad side. Gary Sheffield is and was a traveling show. He hit huge home runs, with fierce swings, in crucial moments, all while looking more bored than Barry Bonds and more pissed off than Albert Belle. Something gives me the impression that lots of clubhouse jokes have been told where most of the team laughed and Sheffield looked incredulously into space, bored by the day. Didn't get the joke? No one was sure if he was listening, but if he was, he didn't think it was funny. The dude was bad to the bone. Call Joe Torre a manager who doesn't respect black players? Oh, Sheff, he won four titles in New York balancing a ton of egos, putting the team first, and making all the right moves, regardless of credentials, salary, or color. Not a great target to battle in the court of public opinion. I'm actually not sure Sheff knew that the Yanks won four titles before he got there.

Sheff was the 19-year-old nephew of Doc Gooden on the Brewers, but he wanted out. He goes to San Diego and almost wins the Triple Crown. He then goes to the Marlins and wins a World Series. Do you remember that season? It was 1997. Lots of folks missed it. Mark McGwire, Sammy Sosa, and the 1998 Yankees would bring back most wayward fans the next season, but 1997 was solidly in the dark haze of a poststrike malaise.

But in the 1997 playoffs, Gary Sheffield was in a zone. He reminded me of Todd Carter. That name means nothing to you. From seven-year-old T-ball to 12-year-old Little

BAT WAGGLE — FRONT VIEW

I can't imitate this ferocious bat waggle with a real bat

League, a kid named Todd Carter played against me. I played third base, and my dad wanted me to play even with the base or closer to guard against the bunt. But for Todd Carter, who hit the ball unusually hard, he gave me the nod to play almost on the outfield grass. Gary Sheffield hit the ball on a line harder than Todd Carter. I can't imagine playing third base during the 1997 postseason. His home runs were the opposite of Dave Kingman's. Sheffield's would start low and only rise. I swear he hit home runs that third basemen would almost catch in the infield. Absolute ropes.

Sheffield is the main reason I use a plastic bat for my imitations. His violent pre-swing bat waggle is impossible unless you can bench-press 300 pounds. I'd look like a 12-year-old if I tried to wave a real wooden bat like Sheffield. The combination of that hummingbird bat motion, the murderous scowl, the vigorous chaw chewing and spitting, and the fastest and most violent swing in baseball history puts Sheffield near the top of stance mountain.

If someone does show Sheffield this book or if he decides to pick it up on his own because of its eye-catching and mildly seductive cover, I'd say this:

Sheff, you ripped the cover off the ball for your entire career. You dominated in crucial moments, you swung the most violent stick in the bigs while not being violent off the field. It's tough to be so focused and fierce on the field, then gentle off field. Way to go. Congratulations on hitting 500-plus home runs.

BAT WAGGLE—SIDE VIEW

Do I look
ANGRY?

From the knees down, the side view doesn't look that menacing

Can you check your swing when you've emotionally committed this much?

If it's not obvious, he pulled EVERYTHING

GARY SHEFFIELD ANGER CHART

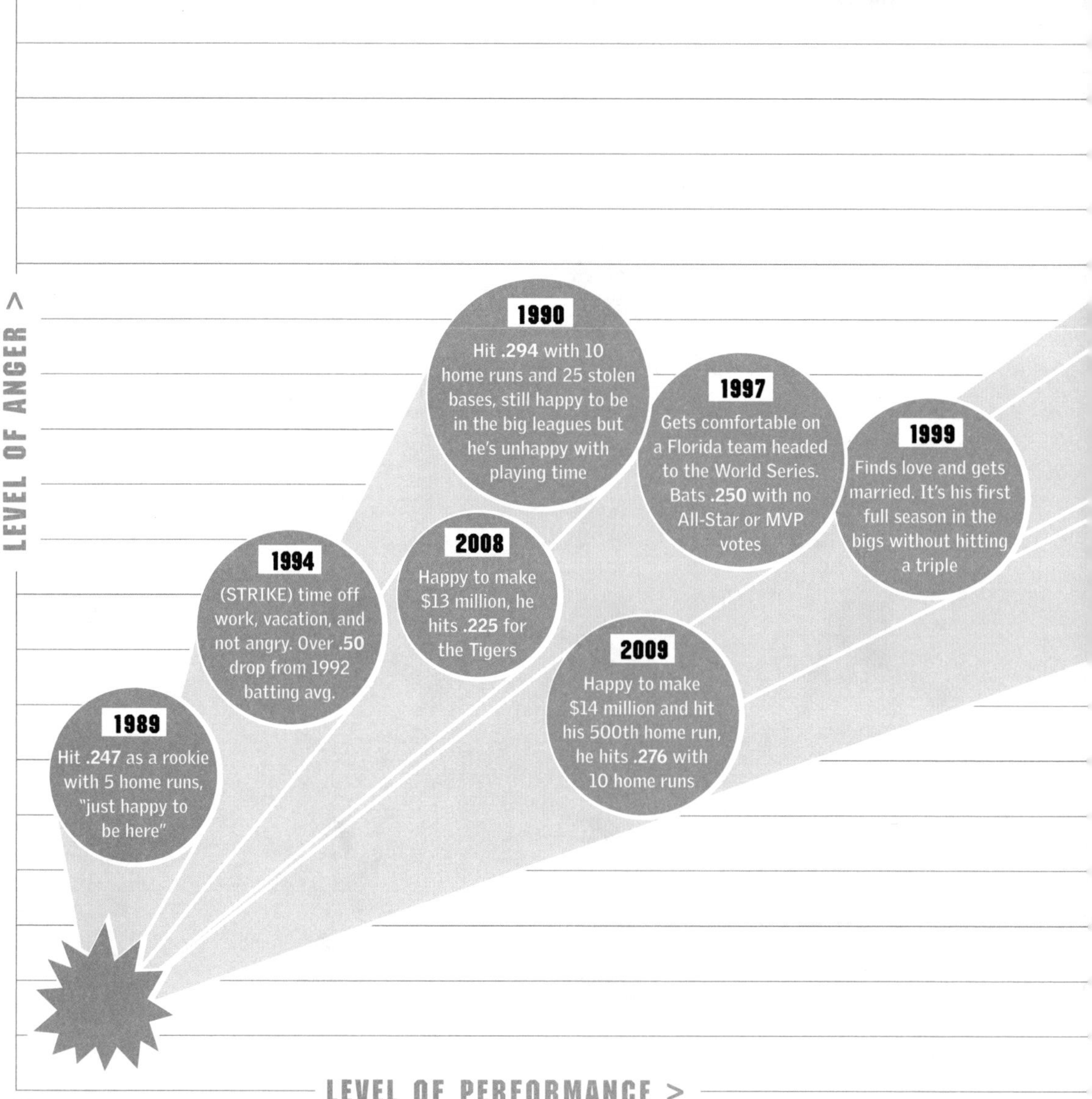
LEVEL OF ANGER >
1989
Hit .247 as a rookie with 5 home runs, "just happy to be here"
1994
(STRIKE) time off work, vacation, and not angry. Over .50 drop from 1992 batting avg.
1990
Hit .294 with 10 home runs and 25 stolen bases, still happy to be in the big leagues but he's unhappy with playing time
2008
Happy to make $13 million, he hits .225 for the Tigers
1997
Gets comfortable on a Florida team headed to the World Series. Bats .250 with no All-Star or MVP votes
2009
Happy to make $14 million and hit his 500th home run, he hits .276 with 10 home runs
1999
Finds love and gets married. It's his first full season in the bigs without hitting a triple
LEVEL OF PERFORMANCE >

1992

33 home runs, 100 RBIs, batting .330 for the Padres. Angry and feeling slighted, Sheff wants to show Brewers they shouldn't have picked Bill Spiers for SS over Sheff

1995

Angry about being injured. Hits **.324** in 63 games

1996

Too many parking tickets and the series finales of *The Fresh Prince of Bel-Air* and *Murder, She Wrote* leave Gary angry and empty feeling. He leads the league in on-base percentage, hits **.314** with 42 home runs and 120 RBIs

1998

Gets traded to the Dodgers for Mike Piazza. Pissed! Hits over **.300** every year in L.A.

2002

He's traded to Braves, Dodgers did him wrong. Hits over **.300** with 25 home runs

2004

He's pissed that the Braves didn't re-sign him. He's a runner-up for AL MVP with Yankees

LEVEL OF PERFORMANCE >

MY THOUGHTS ABOUT

THE FLORIDA MARLINS *and* JOE ROBBIE STADIUM

Miami, Florida / Land Shark Stadium:
The closest I've ever seen anyone come to getting seriously injured while texting was during Braves batting practice in Miami. Here are the two Adam LaRoche batting-practice bombs we came away with. The one in my dad's hand almost killed him.

Marlin fans in 1998 must have looked at the team they married the year before and immediately considered an annulment. It's fair to say that they woke up in 1998 and knew they'd be able to convince a judge or priest or the pope that it wasn't the team they'd married. In 1997 it was a beautiful wedding for fans in Florida. A lovely ceremony with Moises Alou, Gary Sheffield, and Kevin Brown as groomsmen and Jim Leyland as the father-in-law led to a spectacular wedding night just five years into the franchise's existence. "Till death do us part" sounded like a dream. Sadly, ownership sold off every spare part in 1998 and the Marlins lost 108 games, becoming the only World Champ to follow up a title season with the worst record in baseball.

I don't know how many Marlins fans stayed married to the team after that year, but if they did, they were rewarded for trying to make it work. During the massive fire sale of 1998 the Marlins acquired young Derrek Lee and A. J. Burnett, and selected Josh Beckett with their top pick. They added Carl Pavano, Brad Penny, Dontrelle Willis, Mike Lowell, Juan Pierre, Alex Gonzalez, Luis Castillo, and Ivan Rodriguez to the roster and won another ring in 2003. That team used youth, youth, and their secret weapon, youth, to shock the baseball world and win it all. In the greatest free-agent signing in my memory, Ivan Rodriguez willed that young team through every round of the playoffs. He held on to the ball after getting run over by J. T. Snow in the NLDS, helping the Marlins become the first team ever to win a postseason series with the tying runner being thrown out at the plate to end a game.

Marlins fans have not experienced something that just about every other fan in baseball has felt: postseason loss. It really is feast or famine with them. They either miss the postseason entirely or win it all, never having lost a postseason series.

My hunch is that the Marlins marriage is finally stabilizing. The current Marlins roster, led by Hanley Ramirez, looks almost good enough to make it to the postseason and not win it all. I'm sure Marlins fans will finally start to feel what Braves, Angels, and Indians fans have been feeling for years: postseason mediocrity. The marriage counseling is working. Marlins ownership has stopped drinking and gambling, and the fans are learning to accept their safe, stable, middle-class life of Saturday nights at Applebee's and trips to Costco.

In July 2009, the Marlins broke ground on a new stadium, a further indication that the marriage is working. Land Shark Stadium, aka Joe Robbie Stadium, aka Pro Player Stadium, aka insert future naming rights here Stadium is lame for baseball. I'm not sure there's any way for mixed-use stadiums not to disappoint. It's not a coincidence that there are only three football/baseball stadiums left in the major leagues and that all three house small-market teams just trying to compete. The Twins open their new stadium in 2010 and the Marlins' new stadium will be done in 2012, which will leave only the A's as a baseball team with a mixed-use field. The new Marlins' stadium will have a retractable roof, something that's great news for Florida fans, since it rains at some point every day in South Florida. Ah, matrimony.

I think these seats cost less than half of what Cubs bleacher seats cost. Marlins fever. Catch it.

topps
MICKEY TETTLETON
Tigers™

MICKEY TETTLETON

THERE HAVE BEEN PLAYERS WHO HELD THEIR BATS PRECARIOUSLY HORIZONTAL. THERE HAVE BEEN PLAYERS WHO STOOD STRAIGHT UP. THERE HAVE BEEN PLAYERS WHO UNBUTTONED THEIR JERSEYS ONE BUTTON TOO MANY LIKE A GUEST STAR ON *MIAMI VICE*.

There have been players with an inordinate amount of chaw in their mouths. There have been players who featured an all-business steely glare at the pitcher. There have even been players who appeared to be able to bench-press 400 pounds.

There is only one player who put all that together and formed a company called Mickey Tettleton. That company was about one thing: cool. Badass cool. You are toast cool. Check me out cool. I'm tougher than you cool. And yet he's Richard Grieco in

If Looks Could Kill. All the elements of cool are present, but they don't mix well. Tettleton never had the numbers to match the persona. Sure, he hit over 30 home runs four times, but he hit .241 for his career. If he was such a badass, how did José Valentin have more career homers than he did? For being so tough, why did four different teams get rid of him?

None of that matters now, because in my book—in *this* book—he is awesome. He's not just about the game, he's also about a lifestyle. He's tough: a catcher and a cowboy. You just don't mess with him. He's a combination of Chuck Norris and "the most interesting man in the world" from those beer commercials. No one has ever heard Tettleton utter a word, but he knows how to say "I will break you" in fifteen languages, including sign language. No one has seen his handwriting, but we all know his penmanship is impeccable. Rumor has it that he used to ride a horse to the stadium in Detroit. We don't know if he's single or married to fifteen women, but we do know he's attractive to both sexes. He's Tettleton. Don't ever look at him in the face, because his looks literally do kill. Neighborhood kids lose their Frisbees on his roof and know better than to knock on his door. He only eats meat, and only if it's raw. He only drinks motor oil. He's a clean shave away from being Randall "Tex" Cobb's motorcycle-riding character in *Raising Arizona.* You don't mess with Tettleton. I'm actually afraid to imitate his stance.

ALL-TIME BEST

UNBUTTONED SHIRTS

DAVID WELLS

In 1997, while playing for the Yankees, Wells tried to wear a hat of Babe Ruth's during an actual game. Joe Torre made him take it off because the hat from 1934 didn't conform to team standards. Unbuttoning your shirt this far shouldn't conform to team standards either.

MIKE NAPOLI

With the last name Napoli, we should be lucky he isn't wearing a gold medallion and a pinkie ring.

IVAN CALDERON

Calderon is Puerto Rican. How do you say *Magnum P.I.* in Spanish?

Unbuttoned shirt
and chest hair
Delicately holding
my sword of death

This is a pose meant for opera or musical theater, not baseball

Massive chaw

MY THOUGHTS ABOUT

THE DETROIT TIGERS *and* TIGER STADIUM/COMERICA PARK

← Alex was up

Detroit, Michigan / Comerica Park: Here's me and my dad in Detroit about to catch an A-Rod pop foul. Mike Maroth pitched a gem, and the Tigers beat a good Yankee team.

For a city that's fallen on really hard times, Detroit has an impressive commitment and connection to its baseball team. It seems like it's always been a town that adores its sports heroes. Whether it's fans staying well after a game to reach out to touch Mark Fidrych after an outstanding regular-season pitching performance during his rookie year in 1976 or a packed crowd going absolutely bananas for Justin Verlander when he threw a no-hitter in 2007, Detroit fans are as intense as any fans on the planet.

Any mention of Fidrych reminds me about the loss of personality in baseball, something that on some level is counterintuitive to the business side of the game. Fidrych was known for, among other things, talking to the ball when he was on the mound. Anything I've read or heard about Fidrych's magical rookie year has always mentioned that he became an object of affection and fascination for fans of all kinds because of his antics. If prospective free agents in today's game had any marketing savvy, they'd spend their contract years making contact, hustling their butts off, and acting like lovable lunatics. If you think Johnny Damon got a four-year deal with the Yankees worth $52 million just because he got hits, you're sorely mistaken. It had just about as much to do with the crazy biker beard and "idiot" act that got him the big dollars.

The Tigers making it to the World Series in 2006 was like seeing the Pirates and the Rangers in the 2010 World Series: unfathomable. Sure, they had hired Jim Leyland and signed Ivan Rodriguez, but they'd lost 90-plus games in eight of the previous 10 seasons and had lost more than 100 games three times during that decade. The amazing turnaround made Placido Polanco's jubilant jazz-handzie scamper around the bases on Magglio's ALCS walk-off 2006 home run that much more memorable. It was also the first time I recall a ski mask being involved in a pennant-clinching moment.

A trade I rarely hear about but that seems crazy on paper: John B. Wockenfuss was traded with Glenn Wilson from the Tigers in the 1984 preseason to the Phillies for Dave Bergman and Willie Hernandez. The Phillies won the pennant and made it to the World Series with Willie as their middle reliever in 1983. They finished fourth in the National League East in 1984 with Wockenfuss playing 86 games as a utility player while Hernandez became a fantastic closer and had a 1984 season for the ages. He won the Cy Young Award, the American League MVP, and to top it, pitched the final out to secure the Tigers' World Championship.

I appreciate the classic nature of the Tigers' home jerseys. Even if it's not exactly true, I'd like to think that Detroit has never really changed their home uniforms. The fact that Magglio Ordonez and Al Kaline both look like they're wearing the same home uniforms is awesome. Why mess with something that's perfect? The Diamondbacks and the Rays seem to have a different uniform every year. Heck, the Rays changed their name a few years ago. Imagine Detroit just becoming the Gers. Here's a serious question: why hasn't Kellogg's bought the Tigers and turned the team into a marketing force for Frosted Flakes? Kellogg's is based in Battle Creek, Michigan, so I'm assuming I'm not the first person to have thought of this. They'd be like the Nippon Ham Fighters of the Japanese leagues, but instead of promoting ham consumption, the Tigers would be promoting cereal. Food for thought, literally.

There was a real charm to Tiger Stadium. It was time for it to go, and Comerica is nice, but lots of 30- to 40-year-olds must miss the downtown staple. I sat in the upper deck in center field and felt about 14 miles away from the center fielder. The only place farther from home plate I've ever encountered was the Rockpile in Mile High Stadium before the Rockies opened Coors Field.

This is Andy
SYRACUSE
30
BASKETBALL

Tiger Stadium: My buddy Andy McHargue and I took a lot of road trips together when we were in college, including four cross-country trips from Oakland to Syracuse. We saw 19 games in 16 stadiums during our four years of college.

Topps
ORIOLES
CAL RIPKEN
3rd BASE

CAL RIPKEN JR.

CAL RIPKEN SWITCHED HIS STANCE MORE THAN ANY OTHER PLAYER IN RECENT MEMORY.

Peter Gammons told me Yaz switched his stance every year, but Cal's brother Billy said Cal switched his stance midseason, midgame, even mid-at-bat. He began his career with "the Doug DeCinces," then switched to "the Tettleton," "the Wockenfuss," and "the Vernon Wells."

The most beloved and memorable of the Ripken stances was "the Violin." Cal would bend his knees and slightly open his stance to face the pitcher. He would rest the bat on his shoulder while thrusting the bat knob back and forth toward the strike zone. This movement was widely considered Cal's batting masterpiece.

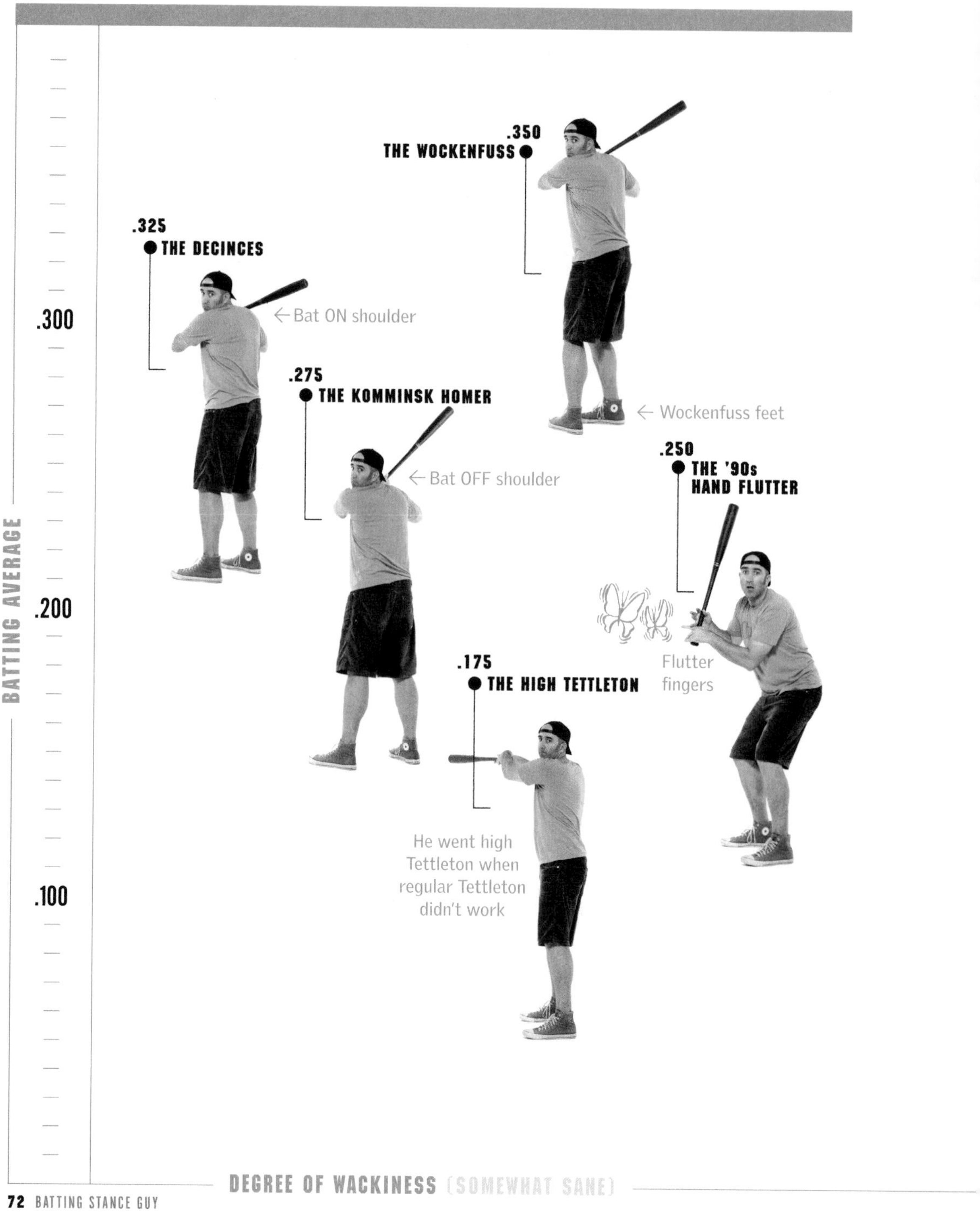
.350
THE WOCKENFUSS
.325
THE DECINCES
← Bat ON shoulder
.300
.275
THE KOMMINSK HOMER
← Wockenfuss feet
← Bat OFF shoulder
.250
THE '90s HAND FLUTTER
BATTING AVERAGE
.200
.175
THE HIGH TETTLETON
Flutter fingers
He went high Tettleton when regular Tettleton didn't work
.100
DEGREE OF WACKINESS (SOMEWHAT SANE)

.360
THE 1991 MVP
Knees bent →
.385
THE DOJO
Special
SUGGESTED STANCE
He might have only → done this in my dreams about him
.275
THE VIOLIN
.250
THE TETTLETON
.200
THE 2001 ALL-STAR GAME
He hit a homer off Chan Ho Park with this stance
Special
SUGGESTED STANCE
His boldest move → in a 23-year career might have been going to the plate with no bat
THE NO-BAT DOJO
.010
DEGREE OF WACKINESS (COMPLETELY INSANE)

I was contracted by Sony to do the motion capture for "MLB: The Show," their baseball video game. They put a wet suit on me with all the motion capture reflector balls, and I stood on a big, empty soundstage with a bunch of weird and probably very expensive equipment surrounding me. The game developers called out the names of batters, and I imitated their mannerisms and plate high jinks. I went through the ritual for each player and began the swing. I would then hold the swing before I came through the zone, followed by a second take, with me finishing the player's swing and running to first base.

Why is this interesting? They didn't have me swing through the zone because almost every player comes through the hitting zone exactly the same. Sure Jim Edmonds and Adam Kennedy look like they are swinging upward, and Don Mattingly and Otis Nixon appear to swing downward, but most players come through the zone similarly.

Ripken embodies that principle. He had all sorts of different angles and quirks for what happened at the plate, the only constant being the swing itself. He began each pitch in a seemingly different position than the last at-bat, but he always came through the hitting zone exactly the same. A stance is the starting point and trigger, no doubt, but it amazed me how at the end of the day, your swing has to be somewhat level with good weight balance and technique. It makes me wonder why so many Little League coaches harp on kids to hit like "you're supposed to." What they should be saying is do what you want; all that matters is your swing.

My wife got upset when our daughter's kindergarten teacher marked down papers where kids colored outside the lines. Ripken colored outside the lines. All these Top 20 players colored outside the lines. And Ripken even unintentionally raised a philosophical question: why stick with your stance? Phil Plantier and Tony Batista had nominal success at the major league level while committing to a wacky stance. When Batista was 3 for 35 on the Orioles, did he consider squaring up and swinging away? Marquis Grissom played 10 years with a painfully boring stance and all of a sudden put together a three-year stint on the West Coast with some bizarre stances. With the Dodgers he stuck his bat as high as it would go, while with San Francisco he hopped around while his bat rested on his shoulder, with the head of the bat pointing downward.

When to stay? When to change? Why commit to a stance when you're heading to the minors? Why incessantly tweak and change like Ripken and Yaz? As my dad would say, "In a bacon and eggs breakfast, the chicken is involved, the pig is committed." Why commit to a stance? I love that Ripken, a man known for being so consistent in every facet of the game, changed his stance more than any other player.

MY THOUGHTS ABOUT

THE BALTIMORE ORIOLES *and* ORIOLE PARK AT CAMDEN YARDS

Is Earl Weaver dead? He's not? Even if he was, the Orioles should bring him back as their manager. He led Baltimore to four World Series appearances when he was their manager and he had a .583 regular-season winning percentage, achievements that make him a Hall of Famer.

When I was young and before I was young, the O's were great. Fresh off a World Series appearance in 1979, they had pitching for days and were always in pennant races. They were triumphant in the 1983 World Series and looked like they'd be good for years to come. Yet despite having stars like Cal Ripken Jr., Eddie Murray, Mike Mussina, Rafael Palmeiro, and Roberto Alomar, the O's have made the playoffs only twice in the past 26 years.

Camden Yards is a really great park to watch a game. It was the first of the current retro parks, and it's sad that the Orioles haven't lived up to the promise of their home. On paper it doesn't make much sense that the Orioles are so bad. They've got a sizeable payroll, reasonable ticket prices, a great ballpark, and Andy MacPhail as a general manager who did good things with the Twins. Owner Peter Angelos must scratch his head every day and wonder what he has to do to win more games. The problem might be their pitching. Despite having Nick Markakis and Brian Roberts, solid young hitters, their pitching rotation is a bunch of young dudes I've never heard of.

There are two iconic moments of Orioles baseball since Cal Ripken Jr. snagged the '83 World Series–ending line drive:

1. Cal taking the triumphant stroll around Oriole Park at Camden Yards thanking the fans after his 2,131st consecutive game became official. The moment was as true and beautiful a baseball moment as is possible in the modern era. Playing that many straight games is a real achievement that will probably never be matched or beaten.

2. Derek Jeter's disputed 1996 ALCS right-field home run that will forever link 12-year-old Jeffrey Maier to both the Yankees and the Orioles. His fan interference and the missed call by the umpire illegally saved the day for the Yanks. I'm pretty sure team owners pulled up tape of this moment when they were discussing the importance of instant replay.

I'm hoping that it's only a matter of time before the Orioles get good again. Maybe they can petition baseball to get moved to the National League so they're not always directly competing with the Red Sox and the Yankees. Watch them win 100 games next year and still finish in third place in the American League East.

LEGG MASON

Baltimore, Maryland / Oriole Park at Camden Yards: Camden Yards was the best thing that happened to baseball stadiums in my lifetime. This turtleneck was not.

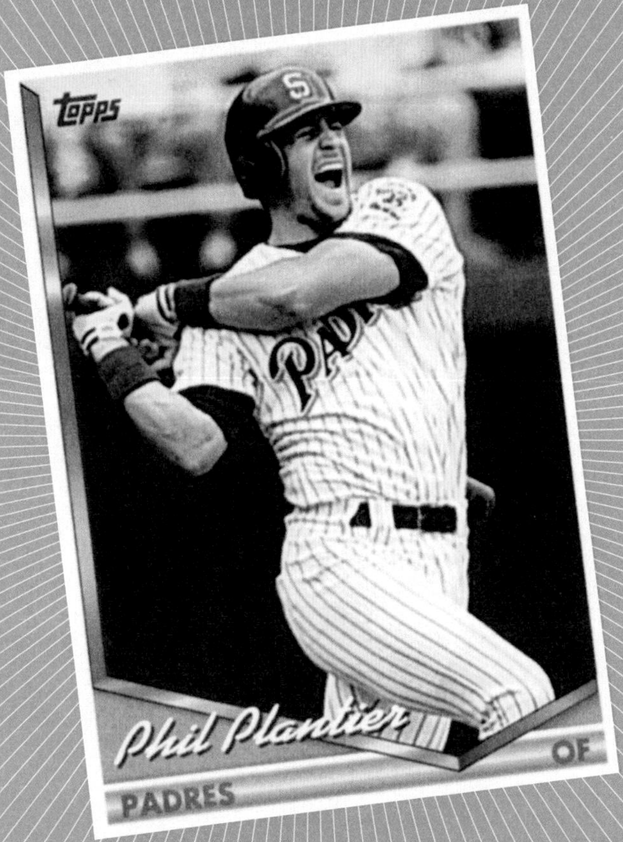
topps
Phil Plantier
OF
PADRES

PHIL PLANTIER

PHIL PLANTIER WAS A GREAT INDEPENDENT FILM—APPEARED IN THE THEATERS FOR A SHORT TIME IN SELECTED CITIES, THE CRITICS LOVED IT, IT WAS UNDERAPPRECIATED BUT FEATURED BETTER PERFORMANCES THAN THE AWARD WINNERS.

Pete Rose won an Oscar for getting really low in his crouch. Well, Plantier went lower. Sure, Rose was a career .303 hitter with 4,256 hits, but Plantier's stance was crazier. He was Christian Bale in *The Machinist*. Oh, cool, DeNiro, you put on 40 pounds for *Raging Bull*? Wow, Matt Damon, you lost 25 pound for *Courage Under Fire*? Bale lost 62 pounds for *The Machinist*. He was six feet, one inch and 125 pounds, a feat that was appreciated only by the 12 people who actually saw that movie.

Plantier had the shortest and least meaningful major league career of any player I get requests for. He had one good year, 1993.

Add another 148 nice at-bats his rookie year in Boston, and that was basically it. Had he stood upright, nobody would remember him. He would have suffered the same fate as Tim Naehring, Carlos Quintana, and Jody Reed—guys who showed promise for Red Sox Nation but never fully delivered. But Plantier didn't stand upright; in fact, he got low—really low. One could argue that the strike zone was compromised when Plantier got into his stance. It's like he was trying to pull an Eddie Gaedel, the three-foot, seven-inch-tall hitter whom Bill Veeck dragged out for one plate appearance as a publicity stunt for the St. Louis Browns in 1951.

I imitated Plantier for Harold Reynolds, and Reynolds agreed with me that the swing was an uppercut. How could it not be? The pitch would have to be eight inches off the ground to showcase a level swing. Again, like many hitters in this book, Plantier has a stance and a swing that they just don't teach in ballparks anywhere, except maybe Japan. I'm actually surprised that Plantier didn't end his career in the Japanese leagues. If anyone can appreciate stance high jinks, it's the Japanese.

In 1993, Plantier hit 34 home runs and had 100 RBIs. That is an incredible year. Any player would love those numbers. George Brett never hit 34 home runs. Joe Rudi never had 100 RBIs. But Plantier was a batting stance mirage.

ALL-TIME BEST

CROUCHING TIGER

KAZ MATSUI

Kaz might illustrate the one instance where keeping your back extra straight doesn't make you any taller.

ALEX RIOS

Further proof that the stance matters: this crouch got Alex six years at $64 million in 2008. Dear Scott Boras: let me know when you're ready to let me help you take any of your clients to the next level.

ALEXI CASILLA

Twins fans must appreciate Casilla and his clutch 2009 single off the Tigers' Fernando Rodney to win the AL Central and seal the Twins' last victory in the dome, but my calves and quads can't stand him.

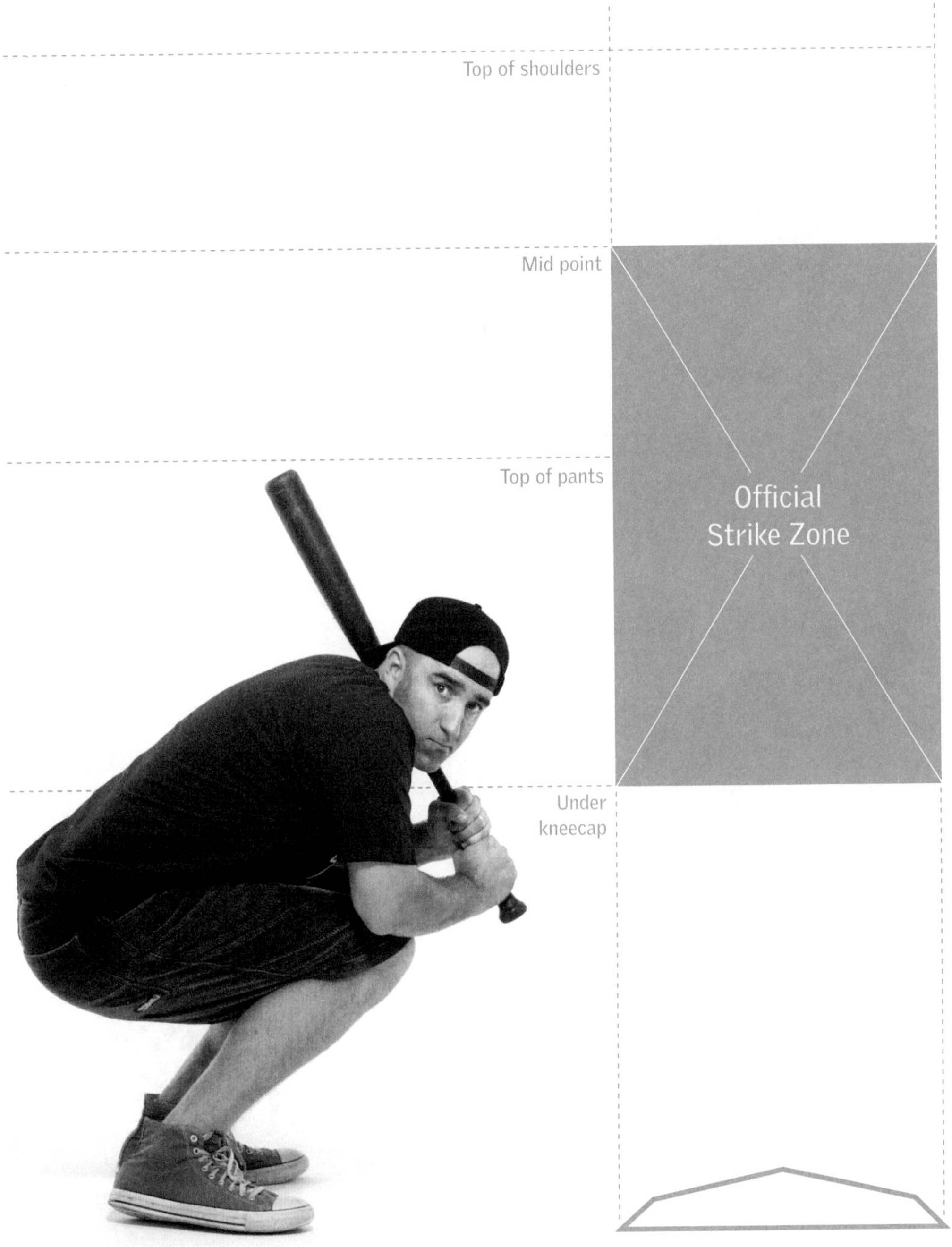
Top of shoulders
Mid point
Top of pants
Official
Strike Zone
Under
kneecap

R2-D2

Eddie Gaedel

Emmanuel Lewis

He tried this during his last year with the Padres. I call it "the Turtle"

MY THOUGHTS ABOUT

THE SAN DIEGO PADRES *and* PETCO PARK / QUALCOMM STADIUM

San Diego, California / PETCO Park: My daughter taking a break from building sand castles to watch batting practice.

My first interaction with a player in my nonofficial capacity as the Batting Stance Guy was in September 2008, filming a Dodgers' pregame show in Los Angeles. We'd just finished the segment, and the Padres were milling around the field, waiting for the Dodgers to finish batting practice. As I'm soaking in the absolute awesomeness of standing on a major league field, a Padres staffer taps me on the shoulder. He gives me a slightly confused look and informs me that Adrian Gonzalez, the Padres' only true star, wants to meet me. I think it must be a joke, because earlier that same day a YouTube viewer told me in rather emphatic and explicit terms that I didn't know the first thing about Adrian Gonzalez. I stroll over to a small crowd of Padres who are holding court on the first-base line and Gonzalez shakes my hand, informing me that they've watched all my videos in their clubhouse. I ended up taking requests from all the young Padres as Brian Giles and Gonzalez looked on. Once batting practice started, I got a chance to meet Wally Joyner, who was then the Padres' batting coach. As I started to explain who I was to him, he cut me off, almost angry. "I know who you are," he said. You have to be kidding. It was like Michael Strahan asking Jared for an autograph when they did a Subway commercial together. It just doesn't quite compute. The notion that any of my heroes both know who I am and have laughed at the silly videos I've made in my backyard is completely absurd.

Like the Expos and Pirates, the San Diego Padres' best players are often more commonly associated with other franchises. Sure, Tony Gwynn, Trevor Hoffman, and Adrian Gonzalez are iconic Padres, but when Padres fans talk about "their" guys, they'll also mention Ozzie Smith (Cards), Wally Joyner (Angels), Dave Winfield (Yanks), Ryan Klesko (Braves), Kevin Brown (nomad), and even Rickey Henderson (what team didn't he play for?).

The Padres' new ballpark is a work of art. I'll wager it's the best ballpark in baseball for kids or for a father in his mid-30s who acts like a child most of the time. You can build sand castles right behind the center-field fence. You can play Wiffle Ball on a real Wiffle Ball field, plush with a fence, dirt baselines, a backstop, and a Padres staffer pitching. Past the bleachers and overlooking the field there is a huge sloped grassy area where a family can bring blankets, have a picnic, and watch the game. It's just a gorgeous stadium without a single bad seat. With nice weather 364 days a year, San Diego is close to baseball heaven.

A book by me isn't complete without mentioning Ted Giannoulas, aka "the San Diego Chicken." I'd be lying if I didn't admit that the idea of becoming beloved in the world of baseball without ever recording a single out or an at-bat is appealing to me. There, I said it. I want to be the San Diego Chicken. Bring back "the Baseball Bunch" and put me in whatever silly animal costume you want, because I'm in.

Sammy →

Qualcomm Stadium: When a professional team has a high school dugout, you know ownership has cut some corners. The packed crowd is on its feet because that's Sammy Sosa trying to hit his 63rd home run of the season in 1998 to surpass Mark McGwire. They were both stuck on 62 that day. Sosa went 0 for 4 with four strikeouts.

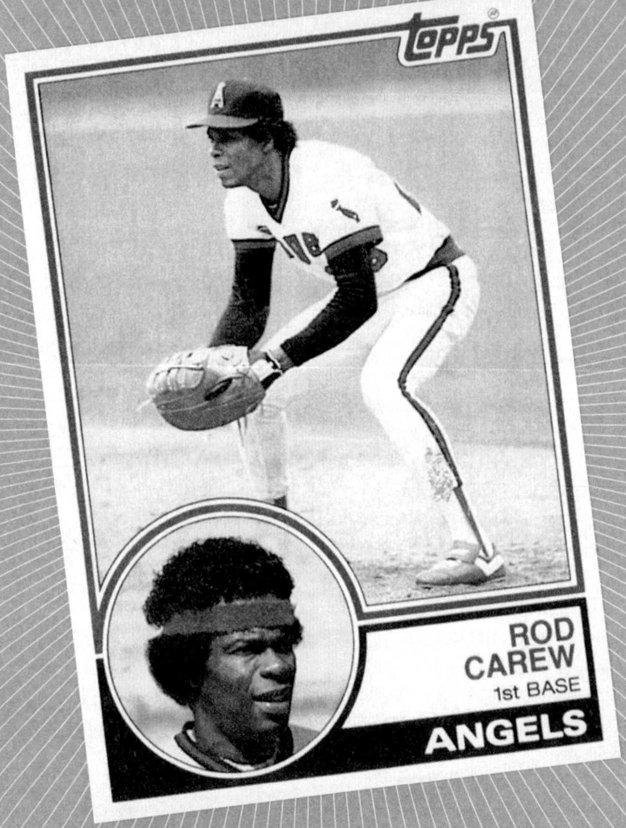

topps
ROD
CAREW
1st BASE
ANGELS

ROD CAREW

ROD CAREW IS THE BEST EXAMPLE OF A GRACEFUL ATHLETE. THERE'S A GOOD REASON WHY ADAM SANDLER SANG ABOUT HIM AND THE BEASTIE BOYS RAPPED ABOUT HIM. A PROTOTYPICAL HALL OF FAMER, HE WAS ROOKIE OF THE YEAR WITH THE TWINS IN 1967, AMERICAN LEAGUE MVP 10 YEARS LATER, AN ALL-STAR FOR 18 STRAIGHT YEARS, AND WON THE AMERICAN LEAGUE BATTING CROWN SEVEN TIMES. HE ALSO HIT .388 IN 1977.

As George Brett, John Olerud, and Tony Gwynn will tell you, getting that close to hitting .400 in the modern era is a remarkable feat. Despite playing for the small market Twins, and being a soft-spoken guy from Panama who basically hit only singles and probably thought home runs were fascist, Carew graced the cover of *Time* magazine in July 1977, the only active major leaguer to make the cover over a 10-year span.

To say Carew was loose at the plate is like saying Bobby Cox may like to argue with umpires. There's a 23.4 percent chance that Carew was so loose and mellow at the plate that he fell asleep between pitches. Like my kids, he'd probably say he was just resting his eyelids, but there were some split seconds in his career when he snored at the plate. He held his hands over the plate and rested the bat horizontally. He held the bat more upright with the Twins, but when he really captured my imagination, as a member of the Angels in the early '80s, he had the bat almost parallel to the ground.

As a player who never really hit for power, I think Carew was a lot like Ichiro in that it looked like he made a conscious effort not to swing for the fences. He led the league in hitting in 1972 without hitting a single home run. To put that in perspective: nobody else in the post-deadball era has done that. Everyone else at least accidentally hit a few out of the park. If you've got the eyes and the hands to hit .388 with 38 doubles and 16 triples, as Carew did in 1977, you probably could hit a ton of home runs if you really wanted to. Carew's hitting reflected his personality—soft-spoken and lacking the flash and sparkle of Reggie Jackson and Rickey Henderson. I'm pretty sure Rod never spoke about himself in the third person. "Speak softly and carry a big stick" is a phrase Carew took to heart, except his stick was a long and thin blade of grass that he delicately cradled in his hands, trying not to crush it.

This is what your 85-year-old grandpa would look like at the plate

BANG BACK POWER

He propped the bat upright before swinging
WARNING-TRACK POWER

I might stretch this to a double
WARNING TRACK POWER

MY THOUGHTS ABOUT

THE LOS ANGELES ANGELS OF ANAHEIM *and* ANGEL STADIUM OF ANAHEIM

I live in Los Angeles and I've spent quite a bit of time in Orange County, the land of beaches, Disneyland, and the Los Angeles Angels of Anaheim. It is because I've spent so much time in the OC that I can authoritatively attest to the fact that it is not on planet Earth. The OC is a land of raised trucks with giant tires, flip-flops, bleached blond hair, breast implants, and a general attitude that can only be described as aggressively friendly and fiercely casual. It is unclear to me if anyone in the OC actually works for a living. Any time I attend an Angels game it's quite obvious that everyone in the crowd has either Roller-bladed from the beach or just ridden Space Mountain.

Angels fans' passionately casual attitude has been richly rewarded in recent years. The Angels organization has put together solid teams that compete. Other than a letdown year in 2003 after winning it all in 2002, manager Mike Scioscia has led his team to a winning record and either a first- or second-place finish in the American League West every year since 2002. They consistently have a core of solid young players who play small ball well along with a few veterans who have come to Southern California in the twilight of their careers. Whether it's Vlad Guerrero swinging at anything that isn't in the strike zone, Mike Napoli unbuttoning every button of his jersey, puffing out his chest and launching his bat after hitting a bomb off Josh Beckett, or Kendry Morales looking like a six-year-old who needs to use the restroom, the Angels have players who are fun to watch.

It really makes sense that the Angels have the most absurd mascot in sports, the rally monkey, a capuchin monkey that jumps up and down to House of Pain's "Jump Around" during an Angels rally. It's genius because it's so darn silly. There just isn't a better example of Angels fans' approach to the game than this. At the most tense and critical moments in a game, especially in the playoffs, fans will go absolutely bananas for silly monkey footage. That just wouldn't happen in Boston, New York, or Philly. In Boston (at least before 2004), Sox fans close their eyes and bite their lips when the team is down two runs with two outs with Papi at the plate and a man on second in the bottom of the ninth. If anyone tried to play monkey footage, the crowd would have a collective aneurysm.

I don't think Angels fans live in fear the way other fans do. They're just happy to be there. Life is good. It's sunny, it's a beautiful day, and when the game is over, they'll get back in their monster trucks and head back out to the beach for a late-night bonfire with their loved ones. It's not like they don't care, it's just that they're a lot happier than other fans.

Angel Stadium is a perfectly adequate ball field. Although it's a carryover from the 1960s, it's undergone major renovations that have made it comfortable but relatively characterless. It was Disneyfied in the late '90s by Disney ownership, so it feels somewhat plastic despite having rocks and trees in center field. Truth is, it's a stadium that suits its fans. It's clean and new and there's plenty of parking for all the big trucks.

Anaheim, California / Angel Stadium of Anaheim: Twenty-two years after I played catch with Justin Speier at Wrigley Field, I'm wearing his jersey for an Angels' pregame show. My 2008 salary had a few less zeros in it than his.

ASTROS
JEFF BAGWELL

JEFF BAGWELL

BAGWELL WAS INVOLVED IN ONE OF THE MOST ONE-SIDED TRADES IN BASEBALL HISTORY. BAGWELL WAS A LOCAL PHENOM FROM CONNECTICUT, ABOUT TO MAKE THE RED SOX WHEN HE WAS MOVED TO HOUSTON IN THE SUMMER OF 1990 FOR JOURNEYMAN MIDDLE RELIEVER LARRY ANDERSEN.

The Sox made the playoffs that year but were swept in the ALCS by Oakland. Andersen had a 6.00 ERA in the playoffs and left Boston for free agency at the end of the season. Bagwell was the 1991 Rookie of the Year and went on to have a 15-year Hall of Fame career, culminating in a World Series appearance in 2005. He and Craig Biggio reigned in Houston, bridging the gap between José Cruz Sr. and Lance Berkman.

Imagine Bagwell, Mo Vaughn, and Nomar as the anchors of the Red Sox infield in the late 1990s. It's sort of painful to think about. Thankfully for Red Sox fans, Boston nabbed the better part of another massively one-sided trade in 1997, when they sent Heathcliff Slocumb to the Mariners for Derek Lowe and Jason Varitek. We all know how that turned out. Varitek may not be able to hit or throw anymore, but he's got two shiny rings and has caught more no-hitters than anyone else in major league history.

Jeff Bagwell hit like he was six feet, five inches, but I doubt he was five feet, eleven inches. In the box, he was four feet, seven inches. Holy smokes that dude let his thighs do some work. There's no way that Bagwell did any leg workouts before or after the game because he did them while he was batting. He'd squat as if he were going for broke at the family reunion limbo contest, his knees spread as far apart as possible. Like Aaron Rowand and Nick Green, he looked like he was sitting on an invisible chair.

Yet the most confounding part of Bagwell's ritual was his hand placement. When Bagwell broke the same bone in his thumb for the second time, you'd think he'd stop holding his hands right out over the plate. Nope. Bagwell kept his hands out over the plate and broke his hand for a third time. Incredible.

Besides being stubborn, Bagwell also belongs to the Miguel Tejada Two-Step Club. This organization unites batters who take at least 14 tiny, little steps out the box before they go off-screen. Other members include Jim Leyritz, Carlos Baerga, and Eric Byrnes.

The pretend ball is less likely than a real ball to break my hand in the strike zone

How did his shoulder give out before his knees?

If this doesn't look comfortable it's because it's not

ALL-TIME BEST

FACIAL HAIR

ROD BECK

Beck lived in a trailer and looked like a roadie for Lynyrd Skynyrd. His appearance is confirmation that baseball players may not be athletes.

JEFF BAGWELL

Umpires often asked Bagwell to dust off the plate with his goatee to save time.

ROLLIE FINGERS

If Rollie didn't have the handlebar mustache, he wouldn't look like a surrealist painter or a tenor in a barbershop quartet, and he probably wouldn't be in the Hall of Fame.

MY THOUGHTS ABOUT

THE HOUSTON ASTROS *and* MINUTE MAID PARK / ASTRODOME

Critics might say that the jerseys of the 1980s Astros were the worst of all time, but I think they're some of the best. It made the club look like they were outfitted by Starburst or Skittles. Billy Hatcher's 14th-inning game-tying moonwalk-to-first-base-chest-puffed-out-foul-pole home run in game six of the 1986 NLCS was made at least 27 percent more spectacular by the uniform. If he wasn't wearing a Technicolor dream coat, nobody remembers that hit, trust me.

I don't even want to look at pitcher Mike Scott's 1986 numbers because if they're any different from 20-0 with a 0.67 ERA, 425 Ks, 3 base on balls, then I am remembering him wrong. Despite Hatcher's heroics, the Mets won game six of the NLCS because they had to; going to a game seven meant facing Scott, a pitcher who had shut them down in games one and four. Consider this: to clinch the pennant that year, Scott no-hit division rival San Francisco, inducing Will Clark to ground out to end it. It was maddening for Giant fans like me to watch Scott dominate, because Giant manager Roger Craig had rescued Scott's career by teaching him the split-finger fastball.

The 1998 Astros are one of a handful of teams to feature four or more players profiled in this book. The '84 A's, '80 and '97 Angels, and the '97 Indians all had stance smorgasbords, but the '98 Astros had Bagwell, Eusebio, Alou, and Everett—giving Houston fans something to both laugh and cheer about. Is it a coincidence that those guys won 102 games that year, winning the NL Central and making the playoffs? I think not. Randy Johnson's 10-1 record with a 1.28 ERA during his three-month run with that team might have helped things, but I'm going to go out on a limb and say that their stances made them winners. Just imagine if they'd called up Lance Berkman in 1998 instead of 1999. I'm pretty sure his gentle placement of the bat on home plate after any important hit would have put that team over the edge in 1998. Sure, the Astros made the playoffs again in 1999, but Moises Alou was gone by then, tipping the stance scales back to mediocrity.

We all know that the trade of Larry Andersen for Jeff Bagwell was one of the most lopsided in major league history. As the story goes with baseball, the Astros returned the karma when they traded Kenny Lofton to the Indians for Eddie Taubensee and pitcher Willie Blair. They also rented Randy Johnson from the Mariners for Carlos Guillen, Freddy Garcia, and John Halama.

When the Astrodome first opened, they tried to maintain real grass on the field. Even I know that doesn't work, but it took the Colt .45's playing on brown grass for somebody to invent AstroTurf and put it in the dome. As a nine-year-old I saw a Steelers/Oilers game in the dome, but it wasn't until 2006 that I saw an Astros home game. Minute Maid Park was the last stop on my quest to see a game in every stadium of Major League Baseball. Sure, the new Yankee Stadium and Citi Field opened in 2009, but at the time I can't tell you how great it was to sit in the cozy confines of Minute Maid Park and realize that my journey was at least temporarily complete. As I put this book together, what's a source of both irritation and amusement is that I didn't take a photograph in the stadium to document the end of my journey. What a ding-dong.

Minute Maid

Houston, Texas / Minute Maid Park / Astrodome:
I forgot to take a picture during my visit to the Astrodome, so I drew this picture from memory for you instead.

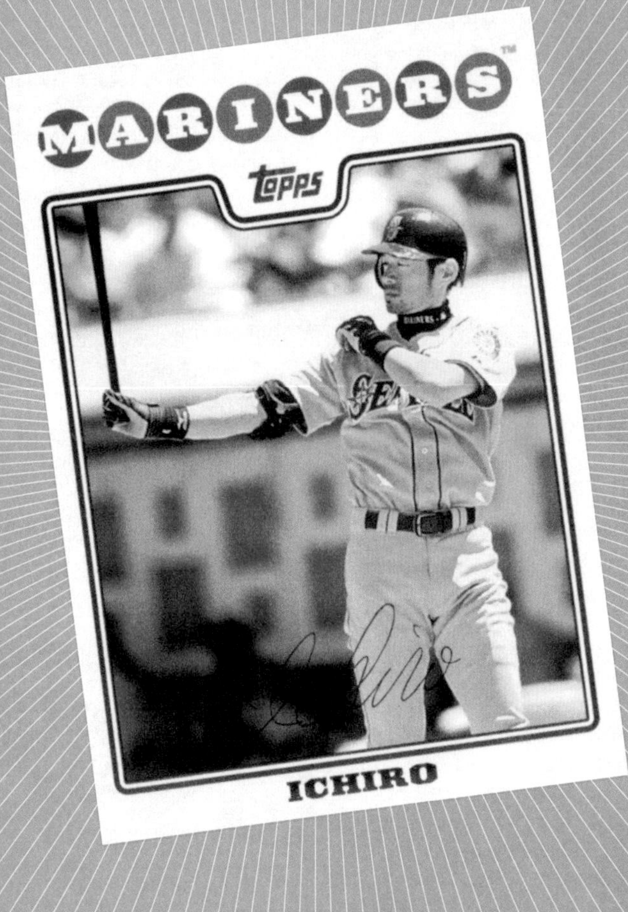
MARINERS
topps
ICHIRO

ICHIRO SUZUKI

SMOOTHNESS CAN BACKFIRE. LEFTIES LOOK SMOOTHER THAN RIGHTIES. WHEN I DO IMITATIONS FOR PEOPLE, ICHIRO'S STANCE IS THE ONLY ONE WHERE PEOPLE SAY, THAT ONE LOOKS LIKE A GIRL.

That's not what I think when I see Ichiro. I simply see a dude who is smoother than all the other players. He might be the smoothest player ever. He's got style for days. His on-deck and pre-swing ritual is incredibly elaborate but done in such a quiet, careful, and fluid way that it only seems weird when you really start to think about it.

Ichiro puts together a "Nomar doing yoga" routine from the time he steps on deck to the time he runs to first base. In the on-deck circle he begins with a Pilates number, the bat resting on his leg. There's a good chance he's doing Tai Chi at this point. He also might have a mantra that a Buddhist monk gave him. This also probably involves Tantra, but I don't really know what that means. Once he's done with this carefully balanced stretch, he squats like a little child, with his butt touching the backs of his legs and almost hitting the ground. I blow out my MCL in both knees whenever I imitate this part of Ichiro's routine.

At the plate, he breaks out the samurai position, using his bat like a sword and presenting it to the pitcher like he's about to cut him in half. It really is a dramatic statement to make to an opposing pitcher. I'm pretty sure he gets away with this only because he's Japanese and because he won seven consecutive batting titles for the Orix Blue Wave before he ever set foot in the United States. If he'd been a kid from Wilkes-Barre, Pennsylvania, or Amarillo, Texas, he would have had all this over-the-top style knocked out of him by his coaches or opposing teams. Aiming your bat at the pitcher as if to say "bring it" will get you plunked a time or two in single-A ball, and just about anywhere else. The only thing that would make Ichiro's routine more absurd is if he motioned to the pitcher with his off hand, coaxing him to throw the pitch. What's amazing is that with the Blue Wave Ichiro featured a more pronounced right leg kick. In essence, he toned it down when he came to America. Ichiro hits singles. One of the reasons he does this so effectively is that he's swinging while beginning his run to first base. He's getting a head start in one fluid motion. He's halfway to first base in the time that most hitters have swung, released the bat, and realized that they probably should start running. Lance Berkman's lefty swing includes him bringing the bat all the way back to where he started and setting it gently on home plate. Ichiro is at second base before Berkman even gets out of the box. I'm actually not sure how Berkman doesn't get thrown out at first on a single to right.

Another incredible element of Ichiro's stance and swing is his discipline. I say

WARMING UP

On-deck-circle Pilates routine

← Finding his happy place before stepping in the box

that because I've been told by those within baseball that Ichiro has been known to wink at someone and hit eight straight home runs in batting practice. Like Tony Gwynn, he's consciously hitting singles. He recently said, "Chicks who dig home runs aren't the ones who appeal to me. I think there's sexiness in infield hits because they require technique. I'd rather impress the chicks with my technique than with my brute strength." Why do I get the feeling that Ichiro is as smooth off the field as he is on it?

Can one player have too much style? I think so. This is where Major League Baseball protects players from themselves. I think that if there weren't rules in place, Ichiro would come to the plate in a smoking jacket and Ray-Bans. He'd be like Hugh Hefner. Either that or he'd be like a young Michael Jackson—weird Michael, not creepy Michael. He'd wear a jewel-encrusted batting glove, swing a fluorescent bat, and moonwalk to first base.

WINDING UP

Note to self: remember to wash wrist band

← Enter the Dragon?

From *Kill Bill* to → *Memoirs of a Geisha*?

Gene Kelly in *Singing in the Rain*?
He's already at first base by this point

MY THOUGHTS ABOUT

THE SEATTLE MARINERS *and* THE KINGDOME

Does Satan really exist? Is baseball really the octagon where good and evil battle it out? I'm just wondering because it seems weird that after an entire life span of futility, the Rays drop the "Devil" from their name and almost immediately win the America League pennant and go to their first World Series. Similarly, the Mariners had a pitchfork "M" on their hats/jerseys forever, and the minute they lost it they drafted Ken Griffey Jr. and became a legit force in the West for the next 15 years. Maybe this is a slight exaggeration. But they did get a new stadium. They went from stray cats biting grounds crew and dreary Kingdome lighting to a beautiful park fit for kings. Just a thought.

I love when conventional sports wisdom fails. When expectations diminish but results improve. University of Tennessee football fans had to be so bummed when Peyton Manning lost to Florida for the fourth straight time. They must have thought they'd never get past them, especially with Manning headed for the NFL. Oh, well. Then here comes Tee Martin (Who? Exactly), who leads the Vols to an undefeated season and wins in the National Championship game against Florida State. The University of Utah's best hoops player, Keith Van Horn, finishes his college career and, of course, the next year Utah makes the title game. Remember when Hall of Fame–bound Tiki Barber announced his retirement? Giants fans shook their heads. "What will we do now?" Uh, you'll win one of the most dramatic Super Bowls in history is all. The Yankees win four World Championships in five years and then add Mike Mussina, Jason Giambi, Gary Sheffield, and A-Rod. Oh, man! Look out! A force to be reckoned with! An eight-year drought.

The Mariners knew they couldn't afford big paydays for Ken Griffey Jr., Randy Johnson, and A-Rod, so they traded two of them and let A-Rod become a free agent. The first year all those guys, and Jay Buhner, are gone, the Mariners tie the record for the most wins in the history of Major League Baseball with 116. This never gets old to me. The cliché is true. It's why you play the games. Team chemistry is amazing. Sure, that 2001 Mariners team lost in the playoffs, but they came together as a team and probably way overachieved. They never sat around waiting for their superstar to save them by throwing a no-hitter or hitting a three-run homer. The Mariners' best seasons have been punctuated by awesome team chemistry and a magical lovefest with the city and fans. That 2001 roster of guys like Freddy Garcia, Aaron Sele, Jamie Moyer, Bret Boone, Edgar Martinez, Carlos Guillen, and Ichiro was just bananas. That team won for the same reason why the small-market Twins won the Central in 2009 and the Rays went to the World Series in 2008. Sometimes a team, despite odds and payroll stacked against it, has just the right elements to compete with the teams that everyone expects to win.

Seattle, Washington / the Kingdome:
This picture is as bad as the Kingdome. This is my buddy Dan Benjamin. You can't see the rats in this picture, but trust me, they were there.

JAPANESE BASEBALL

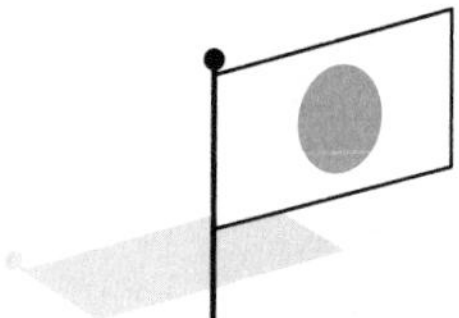

IN THE SUMMER OF 2000 I TRAVELED TO KYOTO, JAPAN.

I was not prepared for what I witnessed. It wasn't the wacky game shows, green tea Kit Kats, gum that tastes like dirt, or the *ganguro* (bleach-haired fake-tanned high schoolers dressed like shiny lollipops with Skittles-looking backpacks and platform shoes) that caught me off guard.

It was the baseball. It happened at a magical place called Koshien Stadium as the Hanshin Tigers battled first the Hiroshima Carp and later the Chunichi Dragons. You see, back then, Ichiro was still an Orix Blue Wave. Only Hideo Nomo and a few other pitchers had ventured east to make the crossover. I didn't fully grasp Japan's fixation on the game. Most of the countries I'd visited loved soccer. But a country outside of the United States full of people loving baseball? Sign me up.

The Hanshin Tigers gave me a taste of things I'd never seen in baseball before. Amazing stadium ambience, unusual pitching motions, chicken on a stick, all-dirt infields, wild cheering sections with well-choreographed chants and songs, balloons launched into the stadium air, and enormous stuffed cartoon animals hand-delivered by sexy batgirls to home-run hitters while trotting home from third base. Was I in baseball heaven?

All these amazing details, as memorable as they were, finish a distant second to one thing: the batting stances. God bless America, the Dominican Republic, Italy, Mexico, South Korea, Bulgaria, Venezuela, Canada, Taiwan, and Texas, but the best batting stances in the world are from Japan. It's not even close. Japan would sweep the World Baseball Stance Classic every year, without question.

It'll take someone smarter than I to figure out the deep-seated meaning of this. Japan's Little League system doesn't breed zany stances. In fact, it appears more militant than ours. In a culture that values fitting in, getting an appropriate haircut, following rules, honoring elders, and not speaking too loudly, the professional baseball players failed to get the memo. I know the pay scale is not the

KAZUHIKO KONDO

Crowded restaurant waiter pose?

same as here in the States, so maybe that has something to do with it. It still feels like a game and not a business. It's still just fun. While there is free agency, it's different than in the States, and players move around less. Perhaps that's why hitters look like they can do anything they want at the plate without repercussions. Wildly exaggerated bat dismounts aren't met with the inevitable plunking in the next at-bat, players fall away from the plate, helmets launch off batters' heads during swings, bats are held in unholdable locations. The country is loaded with Craig Counsells, Julio Francos, and Kevin Youkilises.

While making this list of my favorite stances I realized that many of the players did a

TETSUYA MATSUMOTO

Only in Japan can a player hold the bat like a three-year-old and get away with it

NORIHIRO NAKAMURA

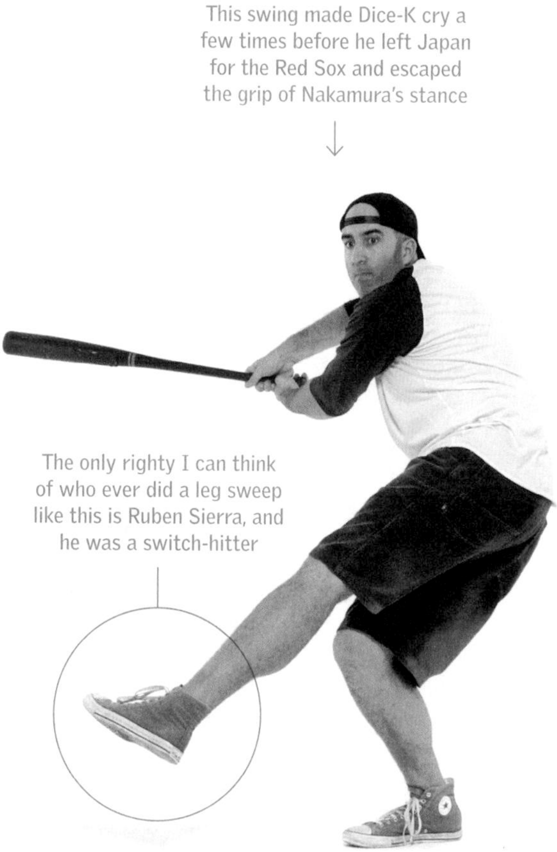
This swing made Dice-K cry a few times before he left Japan for the Red Sox and escaped the grip of Nakamura's stance
The only righty I can think of who ever did a leg sweep like this is Ruben Sierra, and he was a switch-hitter

MICHIHIRO OGASAWARA

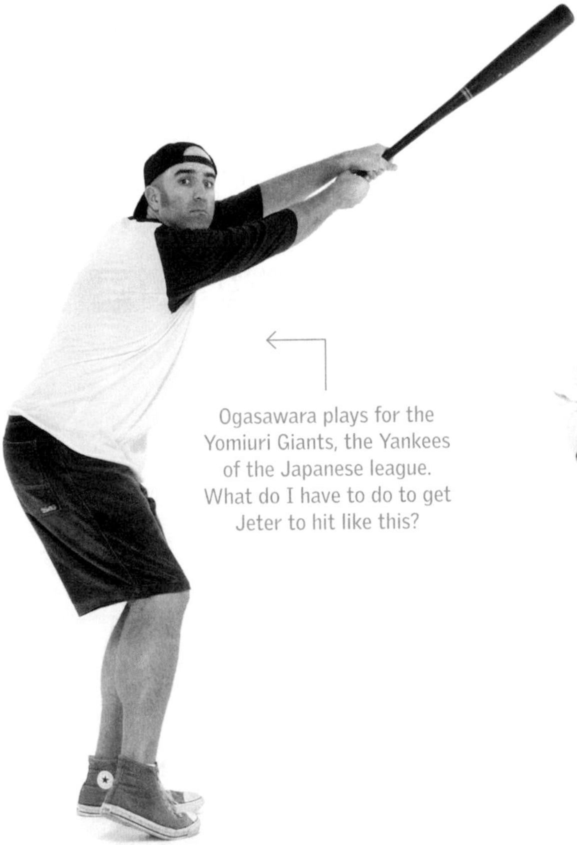

Ogasawara plays for the Yomiuri Giants, the Yankees of the Japanese league. What do I have to do to get Jeter to hit like this?

SADAHARU OH

THE GREAT OH

Greatest home-run hitter of all time...

stint in Japan—Ben Oglivie, Tony Batista, Bobby Tolan, and Felix Millan, to name a few. Even the *gaijin*, foreign players in NPB (Japan's Professional Baseball League), up their antics to fevered levels. Karl "Tuffy" Rhodes pulled out all the stops when leaving the Chicago Cubs for the Kinetsu Buffaloes. He became a cross of Gary Sheffield, Ryan Zimmerman, and Reggie Smith. Whenever the MLB magic runs out in Kevin Youkilis's career, all he'll need to do is send a tape of his at-bats to the Seibu Lions and he's in. It'll be like the band in *This Is Spinal Tap*—once the luster fades here in the States, Youk will continue to be huge in Japan.

When wildly popular center fielder Tsuyoshi Shinjo approached the plate, the crowd launched into a rhythmic chant that sounded like "Cato base Shiiiinjo" clap clap clap clap clap. Every player was serenaded by the crowd, and they wouldn't stop even for pitching changes. Singing, chanting, Thundersticks, drums, and glorified cheering sections. It was amazing. I realized that the Hanshin right fielder was a gaijin. The crowd is chanting, singing, and finally I hear a chant that appears out of place. "Let's go, Tony, let's go." Then I realized it was Tony Torasco. When Jeffrey Maier interfered with Derek Jeter's fly ball and changed the Orioles' fate in the 1996 ALCS, the right fielder underneath the kid's glove was Tony Torasco. Perfect. The Orioles were great in my youth, then they broke up and went their separate ways . . . and here they are . . . big in Japan.

ALEX CABRERA

Cabrera, along with Rhodes, won the triple crown in the NPB and I can see why

HITOSHI TANEDA

I wish that I was exaggerating this. Seriously

TUFFY RHODES

Sheffield bat waggle between here and here

← MLB home runs:
13
NPB home runs:
453

TSUYOSHI SHINJO

From my summer in → Japan, I can tell you that the ladies love them some Tsuyoshi Shinjo

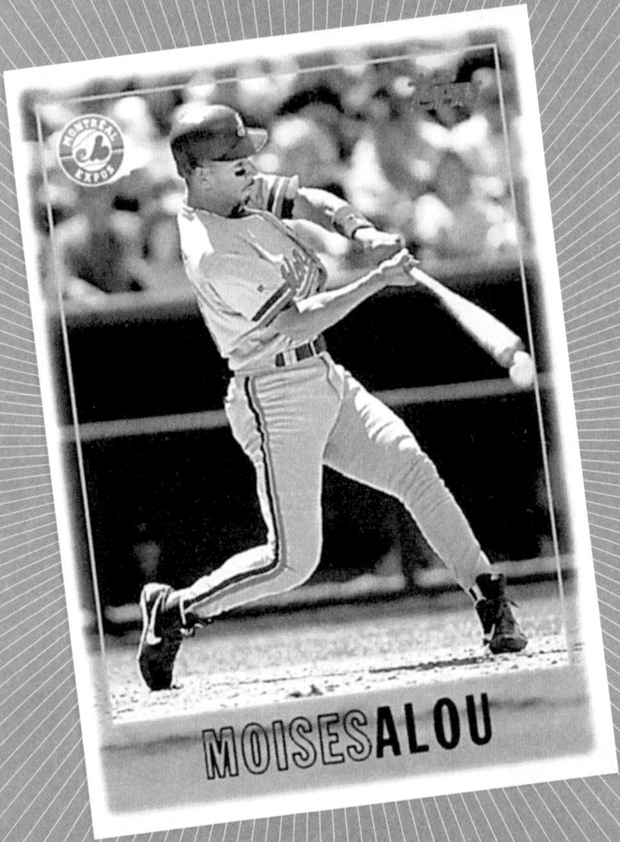
MONTREAL
EXPOS
MOISES ALOU

MOISES ALOU

OVERLOOKED, UNDERRATED, AND FORGOTTEN ABOUT.

For a guy who was a six-time All-Star, won a World Series, and was involved in one of the most bizarre and tragic moments in a team's history, it's crazy to me that Moises Alou isn't on more fans' radars. And that's before we even start looking at his stance. A stance that, by the way, is one of the nuttier in baseball history.

Alou's mistake was playing for seven different teams during his big league career. Those seven teams included the Pirates (ouch), Marlins (bigger ouch), Astros (Enron ouch), Giants (Barry Bonds ouch), and Mets (second fiddle ouch). He also had some productive years for a team called the Montreal Expos—you may not remember them.

Alou could have been the 1997 World Series MVP for the Marlins. He hit .321 with three home runs and nine RBIs to help his team beat the Indians in seven games. Too bad it was for the Marlins. If you're a Marlins fan and reading this: settle down. Pick up the phone and call all of the seven other Marlins fans in existence and tell them not to buy this book. You don't know how lucky you are. Walk a mile in a Cubs fan's shoes and get back to me.

Speaking of lovable losers, Alou did play for the Cubs for three years, so playing off the grid in baseball's wilderness isn't the whole story of his obscurity. He had a career year in 2004 for the Cubs, hitting .293 with 39 home runs, 36 doubles, and 106 RBIs—which you think would make him a Chicago hero for life. The problem is that it came a year after one of the most iconically heart-breaking moments in Cubs history. In 2003, the Cubs won their first division title in 14 years and looked poised for a great postseason

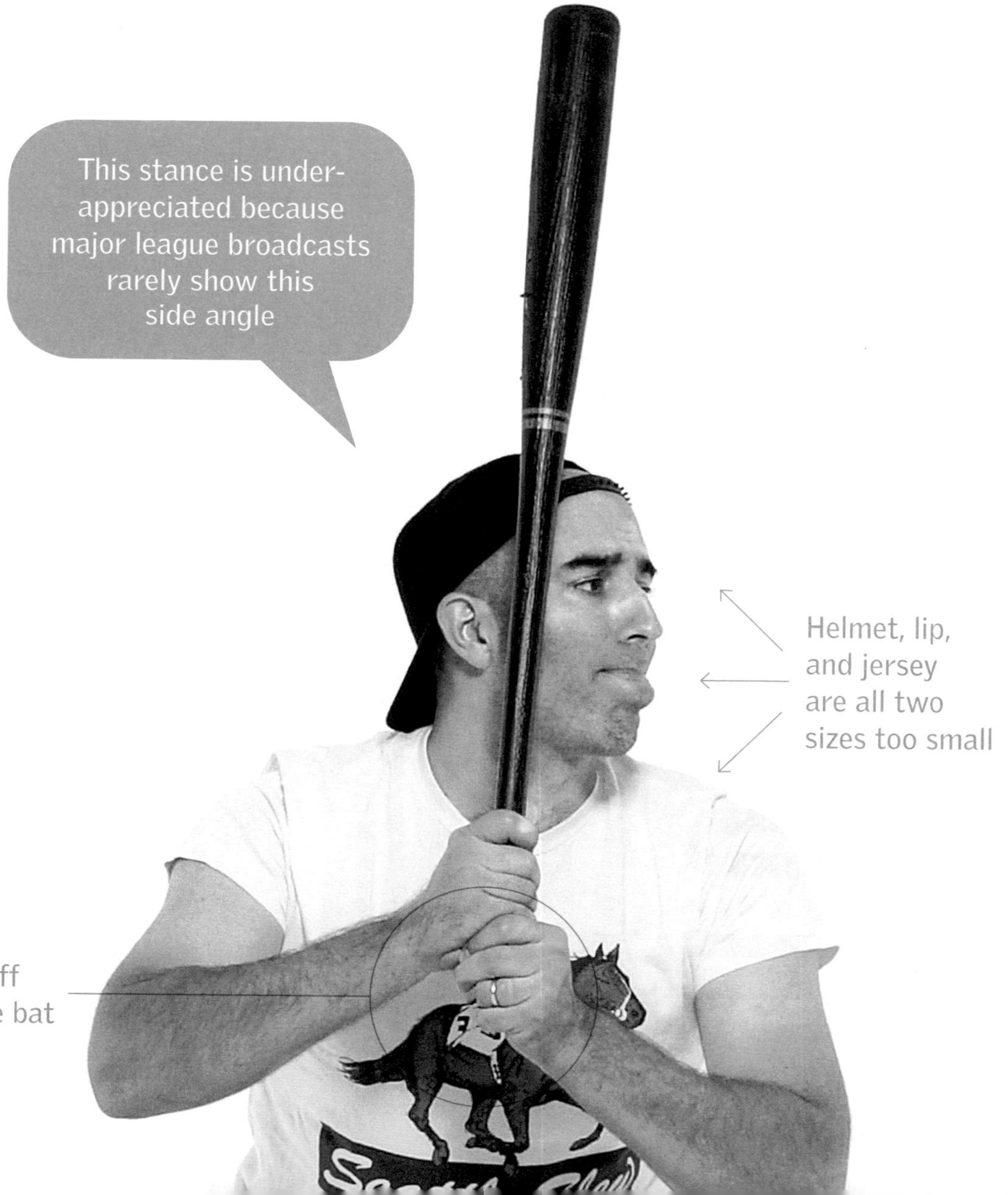
This stance is under-appreciated because major league broadcasts rarely show this side angle
Helmet, lip, and jersey are all two sizes too small
Two fingers off the end of the bat

This just doesn't look cool

run. But if you're a baseball fan, you know what happened: Steve Bartman—whose alleged fan interference with Alou's attempted foul ball catch may or may not have had an impact on the Cubs' ability to get the final five outs that would have sent them to their first World Series since 1945. The fact that Alou was directly involved in the incident probably makes him guilty by association in the eyes of Cubs fans. He's not exactly the Cubs' Bill Buckner, but he's not far from that family tree.

Alou also might be overlooked because of camera angles. Major League Baseball broadcasts don't do Alou justice. The standard front view really doesn't reveal anything zany about Alou. It's all about the side view. His side view is dynamic. He's one of only two players who my wife's friends, having gone to a game and seen him live, have then asked me about at a party. Catching Alou fever is really possible only at the ballpark. First off, it always looked like Alou had gotten to the park a couple of hours late, couldn't find his own stuff, and had to borrow everything from a much smaller teammate. From the chew that was too big for his mouth to the helmet that looked too small for his head/face to a body that looked too big for his jersey, nothing fit.

The stance itself is ridiculous. It's the position my sister stood in at five years old when she wanted to play with us: knees bent toward each other like she's got to pee and bat held too close to her face like she's staring at ants on a log. Alou really never looked comfortable or like he really knew what he was doing. For a career .303 hitter and a guy who grew up in the game with a major league–playing dad, he could have fooled you into believing that he'd never actually heard of baseball.

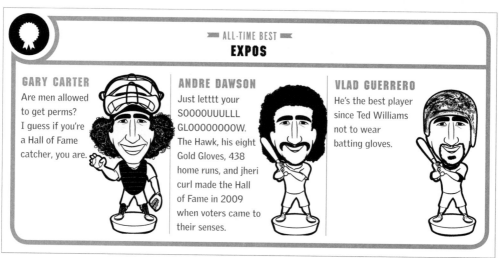

ALL-TIME BEST

EXPOS

GARY CARTER

Are men allowed to get perms? I guess if you're a Hall of Fame catcher, you are.

ANDRE DAWSON

Just letttt your SOOOOUUULLL GLOOOOOOOOW. The Hawk, his eight Gold Gloves, 438 home runs, and jheri curl made the Hall of Fame in 2009 when voters came to their senses.

VLAD GUERRERO

He's the best player since Ted Williams not to wear batting gloves.

MY THOUGHTS ABOUT

MONTREAL EXPOS and OLYMPIC STADIUM / WASHINGTON NATIONALS and NATIONALS PARK

Montreal

Montreal, Quebec, Canada / Olympic Stadium: There were plenty of good seats available for this 2003 Marlins/Expos game.

The Expos were my first love. That 1981 game five NLCS loss to the Dodgers was crippling. In 1983, my Little League team, the Cubs, needed new jerseys and my dad switched the team to the Expos. I can assure you, there weren't many Little League Expos in Northern California.

It's strange to rewatch the footage of the Expos in the playoffs in 1981. The crowd is packed into Olympic Stadium in Montreal. It's odd to see such interest from Canadian fans. I went to one of the last games in Montreal, and I was disappointed I didn't catch a foul ball. With so few fans in attendance, I had a one-in-five chance, so my performance was inexcusable. Olympic Stadium is by far the worst venue I've ever seen a game in. Mixed-use, AstroTurf, bad sight lines, and empty seats add up to one ugly feeling.

What's sad about the Expos is that they had some great players come up through their system. It's kind of nuts that they've only made the playoffs once in their 41-year franchise history with players like Andres Galarraga, Larry Walker, Andre Dawson, Tim Raines, Vlad Guerrero, Moises Alou, Gary Carter, José Vidro, and Pedro Martinez on their rosters.

The Nationals may technically be the Expos, but that just doesn't compute with me. In different cities with different uniforms and no connection to the past, the only thing the Nationals have in common with their forefathers is their ability to lose games. Washington has lost more than 100 games the past two seasons and has finished in last place every year since the move except 2007, when they finished two games up on the last-place Marlins.

One of the lone bright spots in the current Nationals organization is Ryan Zimmerman, who was a non-All-Star with a normal stance before February 2009. Then we met. I did a little stance spectacular for him and all of a sudden he starts doing a hands-as-far-away-from-my-body pose with a huge leg kick. He had his best year in the majors in 2009, hitting 33 home runs and making his first All-Star Game. Coincidence? Probably, but I'm available if anyone is looking for a major league batting stance coach. Are you in the last year of your contract and looking for a big payday? Hire me as your personal stance coach and see the Yankees outbid themselves to sign you. Are your hitters in a slump and looking for a spark? Bring me in for a home stand and watch the magic happen. Your players will be laughing and doing their best Batistas and Ichiros faster than you can say Wockenfuss.

Other than Zimmerman, the best thing about Nationals games is their version of the Milwaukee Sausage Races. Instead of ethnically insensitive meats, the Nationals race the Mount Rushmore presidents. What's awesome is that Teddy Roosevelt never wins. Never.

Nationals Park is everything Olympic Stadium wasn't: a magnificent, state-of-the-art ball field with the retro feel that we're all now accustomed to. I'm sure Washington fans are hoping the notion of "if you build it, they will come" will come true and that the team with live up to the high standards of its home.

Washington, D.C. / Nationals Park: For those wondering where Matt Rumbaugh and Don Buerkle's season tickets are at Nationals Park . . .

TOPPS
OUTFIELD
GIANTS
JACK
CLARK

JACK CLARK

JACK CLARK LOOKED LIKE MY DAD, SO WHEN I WAS A KID GROWING UP IN THE BAY AREA HE ALREADY WIELDED A CERTAIN AMOUNT OF AUTHORITY OVER ME. HE WAS NOT ONE TO BE TRIFLED WITH.

He appeared ready to make me hand-wash his car collection if I threw a ball through our living room window. Seriously, though, what if my dad was Jack Clark? Would he have let me play my Mötley Crüe records? I'm going to imagine yes.

Clark was a slightly underachieving stud for the awful San Francisco Giants team of my youth. I first noticed him when he emerged as the lone power hitter on a fantastic '85–'87 St. Louis club. He was tall and quirky and had a really bizarre stance. He would lure the pitcher into his lair by bashing his forearms together while holding his bat high and horizontal, with the head of the bat pointed at the umpire's mask. He was Mickey Tettleton with a lot more movement going on. Harold Reynolds told me that to keep from stepping in the bucket, Clark would wiggle his back foot. Wiggle is one way to put it. He had so much arrhythmic motion while the pitch was airborne, it's shocking that he ever made contact. And with all the movement and motion on the front end of things, what was more mystifying was his follow-through. Clark's follow-through was like Steve Sax's: nonexistent. Clark would stick his follow-through on his hip and then toss the bat toward the first-base dugout. His swing was the opposite of any good mullet—party in the front, business in the back.

Here's what Jack Clark taught me about life and baseball:

1. You can be one of the most feared home-run hitters of a decade yet finish with 20 fewer career home runs than Gary Gaetti.

2. You can file for bankruptcy but own 18 cars.

3. You can have a couple of good years in St. Louis and be loved by that city forever. You want to pick the right moment to shine. Remember Clark's clutch three-run home run for the Cards knocking the 1985 Dodgers out of the pennant? That was his only postseason home run in an 18-year career.

4. Timing is everything and where you play matters. In 1987 Andre Dawson was the National League's MVP, enjoying a phenomenal year for a last-place team in a hitter's park. That same season, Clark also had a career year, slugging .597 and hitting 35 home runs (the most by a Cardinal since Stan Musial) playing in old Busch Stadium—a park that was never friendly to power hitters. Clark had a .459 on-base percentage that year. Take him off that team and it's doubtful they win the division, let alone make it to the World Series. Clark's importance to the team is highlighted by his absence because of injuries in the postseason that year. If he's healthy in the playoffs, I don't think the Cardinals lose to the Twins in seven games that year. I'm no expert, but I'm pretty sure that Clark not winning the MVP in 1987 affected the voting the next year. Kirk Gibson, who hit only .290 with 25 home runs and 76 RBIs, won the MVP over Darryl Strawberry, a guy whose freakish individual numbers blew Gibson's away. But Gibson is credited with leading a team that had no business even making the playoffs let alone winning the World Series.

Beats Sheffield for
busiest bat and
forearms in baseball
A hot mess
Right foot
squishing
the bug
'85 swing off
Niedenfuer to put
the Cardinals in
the World Series
That's
gone
No follow-
through is
awkward

MY THOUGHTS ABOUT

THE SAN FRANCISCO GIANTS and CANDLESTICK PARK / AT&T PARK

I remember the Giants of the 1980s as a crazy carnival of sorts. Candlestick was the stadium I grew up on, so I still smell cigarettes in 2009 that remind me of the shirtless, nameless man sitting in front of me in the early '80s at Candlestick Park, chain-smoking.

Those Giants had some good players—Willie McCovey, Joe Morgan, and Jack Clark—but they were unusually bad teams. In 1985 they introduced the only home team mascot that was roundly booed, the Crazy Crab. It was canned after one season. That '85 team lost 100 games.

The three most memorable moments of the 1980s Giants included a boneheaded, bare-handed deep-flyout catch, a pitcher throwing a ball wedged in a glove to first base, and an earthquake shaking the stadium in October 1989, postponing the World Series for 10 days. As a kid, it really did feel like a circus.

The Giants of the '90s and '00s were better. They routinely found scraps from other teams that fit well in San Francisco. Several playoff runs ended badly, and the 2002 World Series was a tragic tale that easily could have been about the Cubs or the Red Sox.

Candlestick was a terrible place to watch a game. As a grown man I look back and think that I loved it. That's just nostalgia fogging up my glasses. I love it the way one might love an album by a-ha. It's not good music but it reminds you of your youth. San Francisco has a really weird climate. The 49ers' games in December were warmer than Giants games in July. The coldest I've ever been was watching a Giants game on a windy night while wearing shorts and a T-shirt after being tricked by a hot afternoon.

In October 1989 I told high school classmates that Giants fans were so much better than A's fans. Watching games in Oakland reeked of expensive box seats with businessmen in slacks who drove straight from work. Giants fans at Candlestick had no sustainable jobs, smelled bad, looked like Willie Nelson, and got free gifts from the Giants for sticking around during extra-innings games (Croix de Candlestick pins). Oakland didn't get loud, while Candlestick got crazy loud. BART (Bay Area Rapid Transit) provided multiple forms of transportation to A's games, dropping you off in center field. Candlestick hosed you. You had to drive, and traffic would stink.

I attended games one and two of the 1989 World Series in Oakland. The crowd was buttoned up and snoozy. The A's won both games, and I implored my friends to notice the difference between the atmosphere in the stadiums when the Series moved to Candlestick. My dad and I arrived for game three about 30 minutes before game time. We got up to the upper-deck level, and my dad got food while I walked out to our seats. The corridor into the stadium seating area is the most magical walk in the world for me. Poets Row in Central Park can be interesting, the walk up to Mount Rushmore is impressive, but the corridor in a Major League Baseball stadium where you go from not seeing the field to seeing the field for the first time that day is pure magic.

My suspicions of playoff intensity at Candlestick were confirmed when I walked through the corridor. Loud and already yelling, the throngs of Giants fans wanted A's blood. As I was soaking it all in, the stadium began to shake. I could feel the ground moving, and I listened to the fans begin to yell. "Wheeeehew, go Giants!!" "A's suck!" Holy smokes—I was right, these fans were better than A's fans, and this stadium was rocking, literally. The light standards were rocking back and forth. I saw the foul line between home and third base rolling like a cat under an area rug. I grabbed on to the upper-deck railing so I wouldn't lose my balance and watched things move like I had never seen them move before. It was strange and unnerving. However, the rumbling stopped, and the crowd cheered. "GO Giants!!!" Let's do THIS!!" Having no clue that the 880 freeway had collapsed, the Bay Bridge was falling apart, and that the entire Marina District was now on fire, the crowd was absolutely geeked for the first pitch. My dad returned to our seats with the hot dogs and we started talking about the pitching matchups. Soon there was a strange sequence of events. I could see that the power was out, a cop car drove onto the field, and then I heard the gasps as fans began to huddle around small, portable TV sets. The images were mind-blowing—fires, cars smashed, and smoke from collapsed freeways. Somehow it still hadn't occurred to me that the game would be canceled. When the players' families began pouring out onto the field, my dad said, "Son, they may not play this game." HUH? What? Are you SERIOUS? All the power was out in the city. No stoplights.

THE SAN FRANCISCO GIANTS *and* CANDLESTICK PARK / AT&T PARK

Imagine that. Rush-hour traffic in a city that was hosting the World Series against a team from the next town over and no stoplights? It took us seven hours to get home.

Our biggest concern was a handful of my dad's friends who worked in the city and usually drove home over those bridges and collapsed structures at the time of the quake. But all of them had left work early to rush home to see the entire World Series game. They had all passed the soon-to-be-affected areas without harm and were in their houses ready for some baseball. My thinking may have been flawed but, at age 16, this convinced me that baseball has a magical, life-saving quality.

AT&T Park is a great place to watch a ball game. It's cozy, friendly, and somehow not quite as cold as Candlestick ever was. But it's as if my parents sold my childhood home after I went to college and moved into a smaller, much nicer apartment. It's great and I want to like it, but it doesn't make me feel like Candlestick made me feel. And, like the park, the recent Giants teams haven't given me much to cling to. With that said, Kung Fu Panda, aka Pablo Sandoval, is an absurdly lovable free swinger who makes me feel like a kid again.

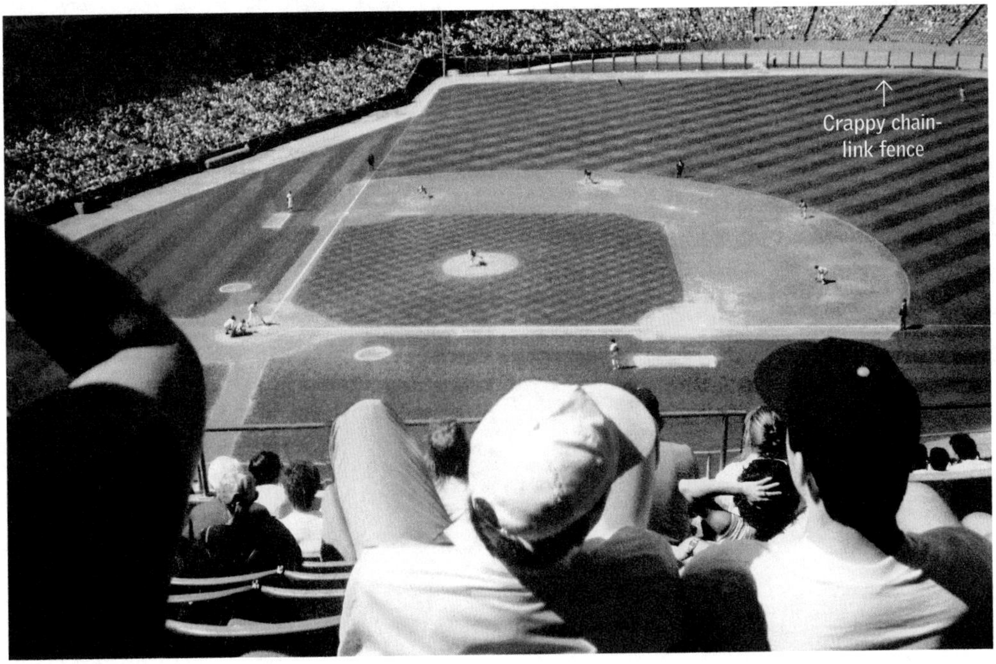
Crappy chain-link fence

San Francisco, California / Candlestick Park:
These seats are really close to the seats I had for the 1989 World Series earthquake game. We had a better fence in Little League than the chain-link fence in the outfield at Candlestick.

NOV. 22 SPORTS EXTRA 1975
YANKEES TAKE GAMBLE ON OSCAR
OUTFIELD
OSCAR GAMBLE

OSCAR GAMBLE

THERE ARE THREE REASONS WHY OSCAR GAMBLE IS IN THIS BOOK:

1. HIS NAME. Oscar. Gamble. It just sounds made up. Los Angeles has weathermen whose names are Dallas Raines and Johnny Mountain. They're either made-up names or they were born to give you the accuview forecast, and I like to imagine the latter is true. Oscar was obviously born to play baseball or win the World Series of Poker or be an action hero. When your name is George Allison Ryness IV, you're a little jealous of people like Oscar.

2. HIS HAIR. He could have smuggled illegal aliens through the border in that Afro. It really was an amazing sight. I don't fully understand how a hat can stay on a head with that much hair, but somehow he made it work. If I hadn't seen pictures of him without his hat on I would have assumed he'd shaved the top of his head and just left the side full so he could wear a hat but still make a statement. I haven't had a full head of hair since I was 20 years old, so such stunning growth makes my eyes water.

3. HIS STANCE. Slumped over, bat on his shoulder and eyes drooping like he needed a nap, his stance is a classic pose. Oscar was a little guy, but he did smack 31 home runs for the White Sox in 1977. I'd like to think that his stance had something to do with it. Like a sleepy snake, he lay in wait for his baseball prey, striking when opponents least expected it.

I'm speechless

ALL-TIME BEST

HAIR

OSCAR GAMBLE

Gamble beats out Dr. J., Fletch, and O. J. Simpson in *Naked Gun: 33 1/3* for greatest Afro in professional sports history.

MITCH WILLIAMS

1/3 Billy Ray Cyrus, 1/3 Kenny Powers, and 7/3 Travis Tritt, Wild Thing would have looked better pitching from inside an IROC-Z with an acid-washed denim jacket on, and Slayer blasting from blown-out speakers.

PETE ROSE

If I told you that Rose posed for a 1977 Jockey underwear ad in just his tighty whities and this haircut, would you believe me? Who knew that bowl cuts and back hair could sell underwear?

MANNY RAMIREZ

Manny being Manny involves Joe Torre and the Dodgers waiving their rules about business casual haircuts.

JOHNNY DAMON

In the clubhouse after the 2004 World Series clincher against the Cardinals, Johnny turned water into Moët and cleansed Alan Embree of his sins.

STEVE BALBONI

Helmet on: feared slugger. Helmet off: my seventh-grade science teacher.

MY THOUGHTS ABOUT

THE NEW YORK YANKEES *and* YANKEE STADIUM

The 2009 Yankees season had a feeling of inevitability to it. Sure, they stumbled early in the season, and fans and writers started to throw rocks at them, but as the season went on and the team started to click, it became clear that they were the force to be reckoned with that ownership had paid for.

I'm not going to waste space making evil empire analogies where I compare the new Yankee Stadium to the Death Star and Brian Cashman to Darth Vader, because here's the thing: the Yankees of the past 14 years make really bad villains. Other than Roger Clemens, the team has been chock-full of painfully likable players. Derek Jeter: a class-act first-ballot Hall of Famer who plays hard and, based on his numbers, never did steroids and still put up amazing and consistent stats. Andy Pettitte: gets my vote for most likable player ever to be linked to something rhyming with: performance-enhancing blrugs. Roger should have learned a lesson from his workout partner, who didn't desperately deny everything and pile lies on top of lies. Bernie Williams, Mariano Rivera, Tino Martinez, CC Sabathia, Mark Teixeira, Johnny Damon, Nick Swisher, Hideki Matsui, Jorge Posada—there's really nothing you can say about any of these guys that isn't positive except that they make way too much money. Of course, A-Rod has a target on his back, but there's actually something touching about him finally exorcising his postseason demons and winning it all.

With all that said, that feeling of inevitability I mentioned earlier makes the moment after the last out when the Yankees all dog-piled on each other a little less interesting. You can almost imagine them all thinking, don't forget to act surprised and grateful. I imagine that competing with the Yankees is a bit like playing Monopoly with your older brother. The Yankees really do have hotels on Boardwalk, Park Place, and just about every other property except Baltic Avenue and the railroads. The Yankees 2009 team payroll was about $50 million more than the next highest team. They have nine players who each made more than $13 million a year. A-Rod's salary was about $8 million more than the entire Pirates team, which should put the painful economics of baseball in perspective.

I'm always intrigued by the players who went to the Yankees and played poorly. Jack Clark, José Canseco, Danny Tartabull, Jay Buhner, Steve Kemp, Ken Griffey Sr., Otis Nixon, Toby Harrah, Omar Moreno, Dan Pasqua, Gary Ward, Hal Morris, Jesse Barfield, Matt Nokes, J. T. Snow, Cecil Fielder, Darryl Strawberry, Mark Whiten, Ron Coomer, Raul Mondesi, and Ivan Rodriguez are all players who played far better out of the Bronx glare. Some came to the Yankees at the tail ends of stellar careers, but others just couldn't handle the heat.

The right-field bleacher bums in old Yankee Stadium were classic, screaming venomous insults at opposing players and shouting praise and support to their beloved Yankees. The love fest with Paul O'Neill was really special. I remember the Yankees walking off the field after the top of the ninth inning of game five of the 2001 World Series and the crowd going nuts in appreciation of O'Neill. The game was tight, and amazingly, Byung-Hyun Kim would give up another dramatic two-run game-tying home run soon, but the crowd didn't miss the bittersweet moment of the last time their Pauly would walk off the field in Yankee Stadium. It struck me as both classy and surprisingly astute. Yankees fans are so knowledgeable. They shouldn't be trusted on "Bat Giveaway Day," but they are a heady bunch who know their history. I remember going to a game in Oakland and watching Bobby Meacham hitting a home run for the opposing Yankees. Listening to the crowd cheer so loudly, I figured Meacham was from Oakland and his entire family was in attendance. Someone leaned over and told me, "Yankee fans are everywhere." Impressive.

New York, New York / (old) Yankee Stadium: Me and my buddy Beau in the right-field bleachers at old Yankee Stadium. For those of you wondering, spending $1.5 billion on a new Stadium doesn't mean more comfortable bleacher seating.

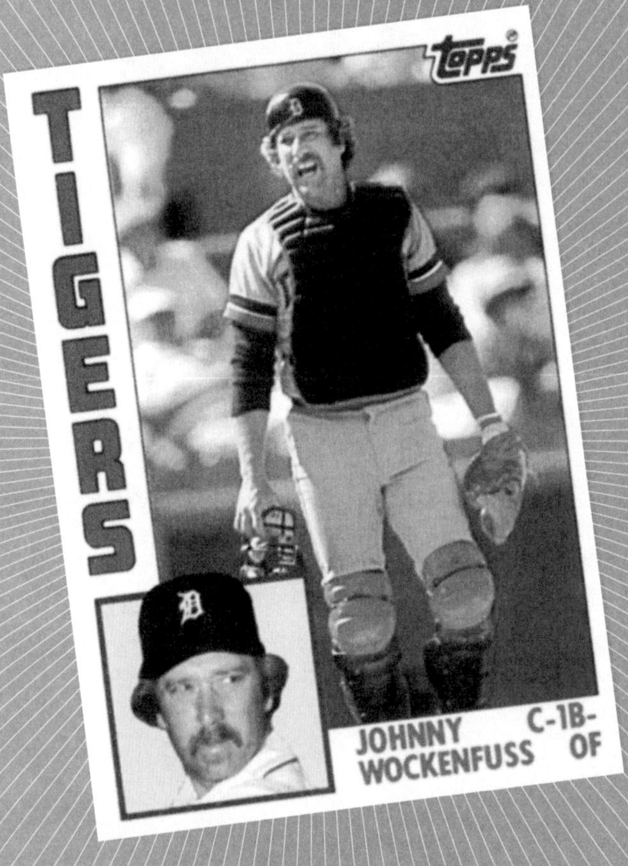
Topps
TIGERS
JOHNNY WOCKENFUSS
C-1B-OF

JOHN WOCKENFUSS

JUST HIS NAME IS FUNNY ENOUGH. HE SOUNDS MORE LIKE A MAKE-BELIEVE ANIMAL ON A KID'S SHOW THAN A BALL PLAYER.

I have no childhood memory of him batting because my baseball brain turned on in 1980. By the '80s, he'd tamed his batting antics and wasn't on my radar. I do remember a series of baseball cards with him in catcher's gear. I remember he was one of the few players whose positions were listed as C-1B-OF.

Cal Ripken Jr. says he based one of his many stances on Wockenfuss' stance—where he would curl his left foot in, facing the plate on an angle. The idea that a future Hall of Famer would try to emulate a truly marginal player is really something. Someone told me that when Kobe Bryant was growing up in Italy, his favorite player was number 8 Mike D'Antoni. Yes, that D'Antoni. Bryant wore number 8 when he first entered the league, so I think the story might be true. I can't say that it ever occurred to me that D'Antoni played basketball, so Kobe loving his game and aspiring to be like him seems insane to me. But beautifully insane.

Along with the odd feet, Wockenfuss did a hand flutter while awaiting the pitch, as if trying to distract the pitcher. It's a classic magician, or pickpocket, technique that I'm not sure worked out all that well for Wockenfuss. A career .262 hitter, he never did much at the plate. He spent 10 years in Detroit but left for the Phillies in 1984, just missing the Tigers' 104-win season and their World Series run, which may have prompted him to ask, "What the Wockenfuss?"

Hunch
+
Flutter
+
Carl Everett toes
=
SOLID GOLD

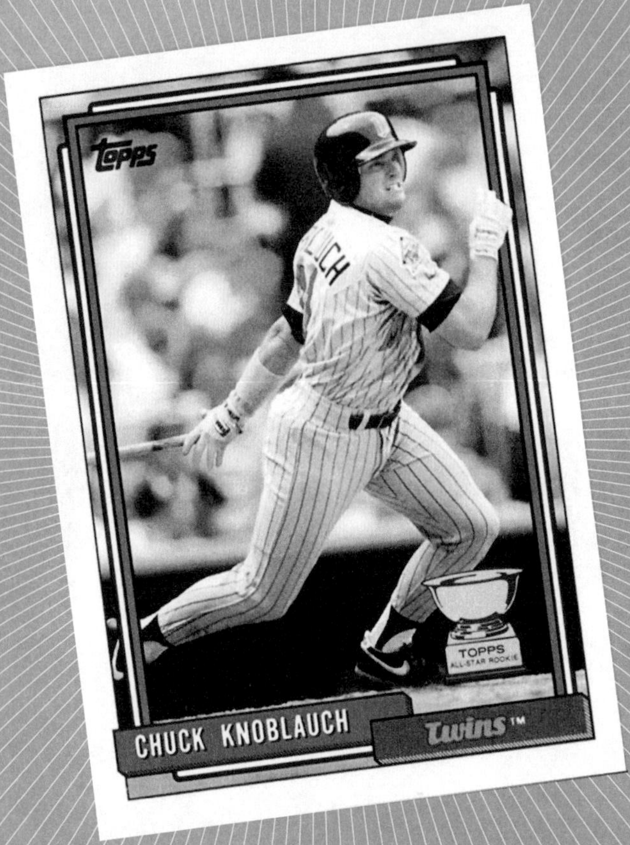
topps
TOPPS
ALL-STAR ROOKIE
CHUCK KNOBLAUCH
Twins™

CHUCK KNOBLAUCH

FIND YOUR SON, FIND YOUR NIECE, FIND YOUR LITTLE SISTER, FIND A NEIGHBORHOOD KID, AND TRY TO MAKE A SCARY FACE OF A MOUSE ON THE ATTACK. FREEZE. THAT'S THE KNOBLAUCH FACE. NOSE SCRUNCHED UP AS IF HE'S STARING AT THE SUN AND ABOUT TO SNEEZE.

As we're building this Chuck character, add the intensity of Tom Cruise. Have you ever watched Tom Cruise laugh with his eyes peering into your soul? Or listened to him scream "I'm having such a good *time*!" as if to say, "I'm so intense and crazed in my relaxing intensity!"

Knoblauch used to adjust his batting gloves with a passion that frightened some people. You got the sense that if he wasn't in front of tens of thousands of screaming fans that he might punch himself in the face. But in front of a crowd he was whispering "keep it together" over and over again to himself. Adding to his intensity was the double earflap he wore in his early years with the Twins. He wasn't a switch-hitter, but his intensity would put him in unsafe situations so he thought he should protect both sides of his head.

ALL-TIME BEST
FACIAL EXPRESSIONS

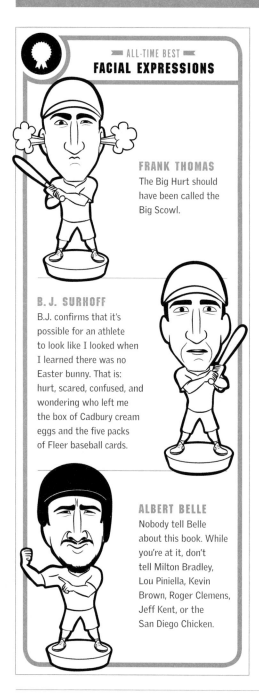

FRANK THOMAS
The Big Hurt should have been called the Big Scowl.

B. J. SURHOFF
B.J. confirms that it's possible for an athlete to look like I looked when I learned there was no Easter bunny. That is: hurt, scared, confused, and wondering who left me the box of Cadbury cream eggs and the five packs of Fleer baseball cards.

ALBERT BELLE
Nobody tell Belle about this book. While you're at it, don't tell Milton Bradley, Lou Piniella, Kevin Brown, Roger Clemens, Jeff Kent, or the San Diego Chicken.

What's really odd is that when he was standing near the dugout, relaxing, he was unrecognizable. He looked like a different guy. Classic Jekyll and Hyde. He'd step into that batter's box and turn into a slap-hitting monster. If he'd gone full superhero he would have turned green and torn his shirt off. Lil' Hulk.

Watching the 1982 World Series, I saw Mike Ramsey pull off his helmet and I felt attacked by his hair—astonished at how big and crazy it was. In 1985 I saw Steve Balboni toss his helmet during the World Series and I recall my surprise that his head featured the classic Bozo the Clown ring of hair. He was b-a-l-d. Maybe I should have hidden my laughter, seeing as how I'm writing this book with a painfully similar head of hair (gulp). Matt Williams was a shocker to many as well.

I mention all this because Knoblauch was surprising in the opposite way. He has a full David Lynch head of hair. Like Brad Daugherty, Maurice Taylor, or Chris Berman, Chuck's hairline seemed to be acceding. Knoblauch scored World Series–winning runs for the Yankees, and when he took his helmet off what was revealed was an astonishingly product-laden head of hair. That hair was parted and gelled like he was at a Los Cerros Middle School dance in 1987, soaked in Drakkar cologne and pubescent desperation.

Pre-stance
finger flutter
Hair gel

About to sneeze
A manic Tettleton with more crouch

MY THOUGHTS ABOUT

THE MINNESOTA TWINS *and* THE HUBERT H. HUMPHREY METRODOME

Great-Uncle
Hartley

Minneapolis, Minnesota / Hubert H. Humphrey Metrodome: My great-uncle Hartley took me to this game and sent me a Homer Hankie and a Wheaties box with the Twins on the cover after they won it all in 1987.

I loved the Twins in the '80s and early '90s. In 1980 I attended a family reunion in Minnesota and went to a Twins game versus the Rangers in old Metropolitan Stadium. The dome, despite its AstroTurf and soulless interior, is a special place to me. My great-uncle sent me Homer Hankies and a Twins Wheaties box in '87. I've never lived in Minnesota, but it still thrills me that the Twins were the first team to e-mail me about appearing on a pregame show. A producer had seen our Twins video on YouTube and assumed that I was from Hibbing or Edina. When the producer called and asked me if I could make it up to Minneapolis in a few days I said absolutely, knowing that it was only a two-day drive from Knoxville, Tennessee, where I happened to be visiting a friend. I drove away from that dome appearance weeping. I'm not sure why. It may have been the song on the radio or it may have been because I'd driven all day and was about to drive all night. It also may have been because I was 35, balding, and had long given up on the idea of being a pro ballplayer or doing anything more than buying a ticket or drafting a fantasy team, so the idea that a team wanted me on their field was a dream come true.

My favorite player growing up was Kent Hrbek of the Twins. My mom would routinely take me to A's games any time the Twins were in town. I wore his number (14) and played first base (his position) in Little League. I figured I'd be about his height one day (6-4) and thought lefty batters were cooler than righties.

My senior year of high school I went to an A's game the night before our first school pep rally with about 60 or so students. We were in the "group tickets for cheap" right-field upper-deck section. As a joke, I moved from the 12th row down to the first row when Hrbek batted off Todd Burns. I turned to my buddies, drawing attention to the fact that I was positioning myself for a Hrbek souvenir. I'd seen McGwire and Canseco hit batting practice home runs to the left-field upper deck, but never right field. It seemed comically impossible that Hrbek would be able to hit one that far. Lo and behold, Hrbek smashes a ball high in the air and seemingly in our direction. I throw my hands up as if to signify, "Dat's right!?" Well, the ball continued to carry, and I leaned against the railing, realizing this ball was actually carrying enough to reach me. I couldn't believe it. My favorite player was hitting an upper-deck home run right to me after I spastically and prophetically called attention to about 60 classmates of its possibility. I didn't bring my glove because we were in a section that shouldn't ever see a home run. I extended my arms and brought the ball into my body to cushion the ball into my hands. I heard a loud, startling noise that sounded like a steel beam getting pummeled by a falling ball. Wait, hold on, my hands don't hurt at all? What was that noise? Why is the ball heading toward Canseco in right? Wait! I missed it. Hold on, no. NO!??! NOOOOO!?!? I did not miss it? The ball did not just strike the beam I was leaning against, then carom off the Budweiser billboard sign below and land in right field? I was crushed. I turned to my buddies and their arms are extended, faces strained, eyes wide, and fingers tense and spread, imitating my flailing attempt. I'd missed the ball by a good foot and a half. I was an idiot. I honestly felt like hurling myself off the upper deck. It was so embarrassing and so lame. How was I ever going to get that chance again? My favorite player doing an incredible feat in front of hot girls and cool dudes my senior year of high school?

I went home, head hung, went into my parents' room and told the story, wanting to be consoled by my parents. Surely they'd understand the gravity of what's happened. My parents got Kent Hrbek to write me a letter when I was 12, so surely they'd know how deeply this killed me. My dad looked at me and said, "Well, son, it really makes a better story that you dropped it." Uh, okay, thanks, Dad.

I had really good seats.

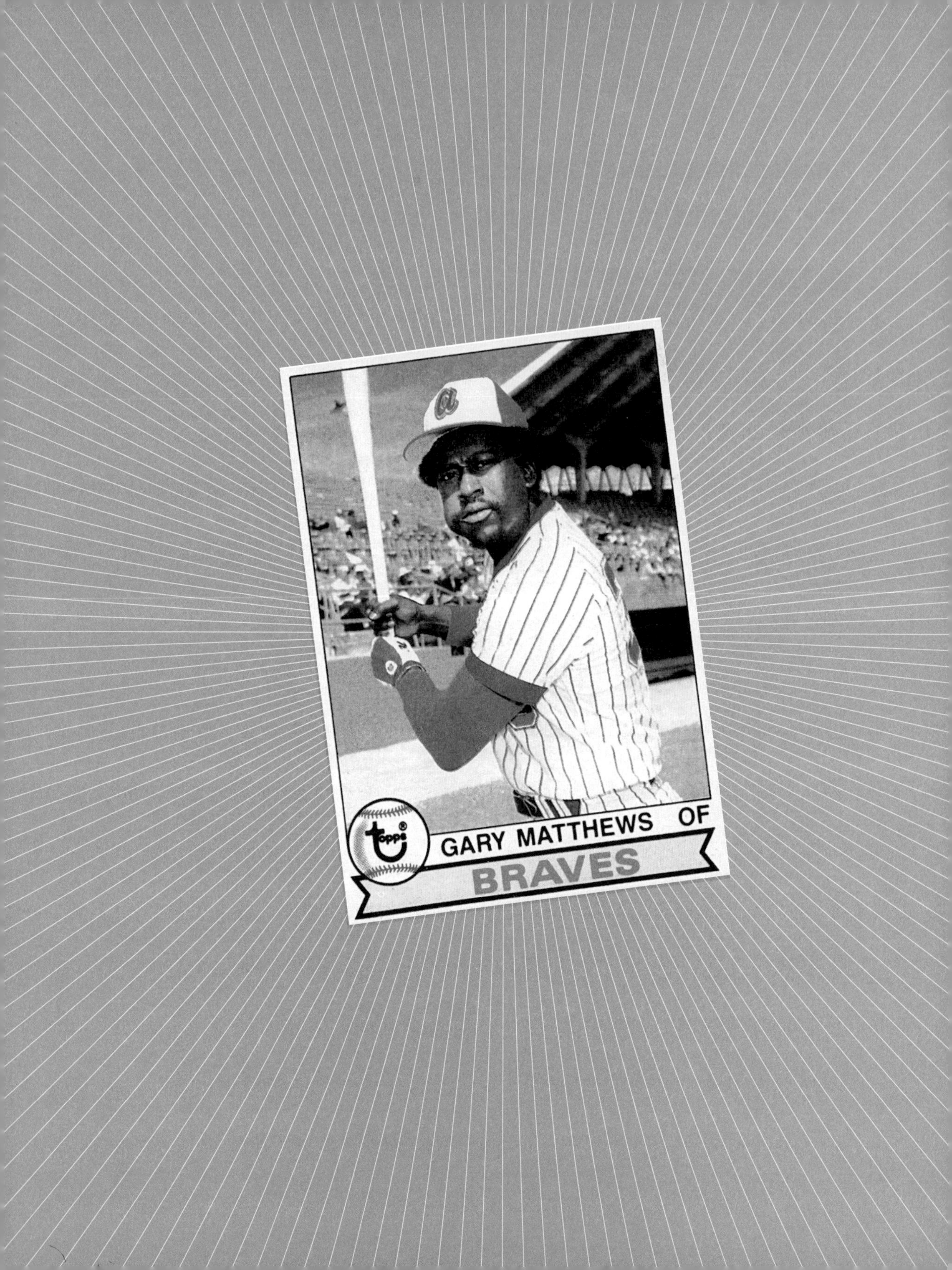
topps
GARY MATTHEWS OF
BRAVES

GARY MATTHEWS

THE SARGE'S STANCE WAS A MASTERPIECE. THE PRE-PITCH SHIMMYING OF THE SHOULDERS, THE MID-PITCH LOOP, THE FREAKISH DISMOUNT, AND THE PRANCE TO FIRST BASE ADDED UP TO A WHOLE LOT OF FUN.

I really never thought a guy nicknamed "the Sarge" would have all that going on. A guy named "the Sarge" seems like he'd be all business. He might have a pissed-off look in his eye like Lou Gossett Jr. in *An Officer and a Gentleman* but he's no-nonsense.

How does this guy *never* get mentioned when I'm imitating stances? He's the Robin Wright of baseball. That woman is *never* on any list of the hottest women in Hollywood. *Never.* Not top 10, not top 20. I know it's been a while since she was Princess Buttercup, and her role in Forrest Gump as Jenny wasn't exactly endearing, but Robin is underrated. A roomful of dudes will always pick Pamela Anderson, Megan Fox, Jessica Simpson, Angelina Jolie . . . blah, blah, blah. Robin Wright does it for me more than any of those other lovely ladies. Gary and Robin—higher in my book than everyone else.

I might love Matthews most because he was clutch on the biggest stage. In 19 postseason games, he hit seven homers, including three in the '83 NLCS. In game one of the controversial 1984 NLCS, he hit two homers for the Cubs.

Beloved in numerous towns, he currently does color commentary for the Phillies' TV broadcast, and fans love his home-run call—"It's Cadillac time, see ya later!" The Sarge's last career at-bat might sum up his whole career. He singled off "Wild Thing" Mitch Williams. What a perfect way to end a career. Moments later, he was picked off first to end the game. Cadillac time, Sarge, see ya later.

PRE-PITCH SHOULDER SHIMMY

← shoulders closed

← shoulders open

mid-pitch loop
'70s toe tap
← '83 NLCS homer
His bat really → was piping hot in the postseason

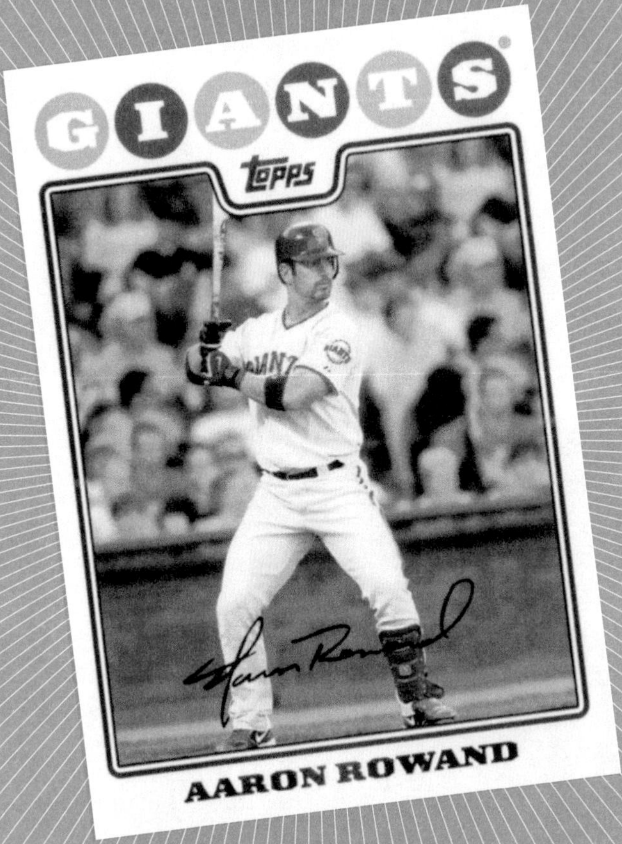
GIANTS
topps
AARON ROWAND

AARON ROWAND

AARON ROWAND HAS ONE OF THOSE RARE STANCES THAT LOOKS BANANAS FROM ANY ANGLE.

Stand beside him and you'll notice that his left leg is bent awkwardly and that he's got an unnaturally long neck that he extends like an ostrich and flexes like Ryan Ludwick or "the Macho Man" Randy Savage snapping into a Slim Jim. Stand in front of Rowand with the pitcher and you'll see that he's squatting like he's sitting on the invisible chair Jeff Bagwell gave him when he retired, only the seat is set higher. Stand in the on-deck circle and catch the side view and be confused by his oddly low hand and bat placement that sits down near his hip like Gary Roenicke. It all sort of looks like he's trying to mimic Japan's Hitoshi Taneda (see p. 104).

The same fluidity and smoothness that Rowand showed us when he broke his nose crashing into Philly's center-field fence to run down a Xavier Nady line drive is on display when he bats. It looks unusually clunky and rigid. Unfluid. Is unfluid a word? Not fluid. He looks like I write. He looks a lot like Number Five from *Short Circuit* trying to imitate Hitoshi Taneda.

I know that all these elements might paint a really ugly picture. Well, it's the opposite. Rowand has painted a masterpiece. He's the everyman of this book, the working-class hero. Rickey's too fast, Carew's too smooth, Cal's too presidential, and Mo's too hoop-earringy. Rowand is all of us. He's awkward. He's the guy who played center field on your IM softball team but who you didn't trust

Aaron: If you have an unusually long neck, this is not the stance you should employ

in left field. That may be why he's popular. In Chicago and Philly, fans loved him. He won a ring for the White Sox in 2005, so that always helps. He also won a Gold Glove in 2007 for the Phillies, validation that awkwardness can be effective and richly rewarded. In San Francisco he signed a big contract and has underperformed. But maybe it's okay, because with numbers like his, he probably never did steroids. He's a career .280 hitter who never hit more than 27 home runs in a season. That's something baseball fans are slowly starting to appreciate as we look back on our past and present heroes.

Topps
Mo Vaughn
1B — BOSTON RED SOX

MO VAUGHN

I HAVE THIS PROBABLY FALSE NOTION IN MY HEAD THAT MOST OF THE PLAYERS AT THE TOP OF MY ALL-TIME STANCE LIST HAVE AT LEAST SOME AWARENESS OF WHAT THEY DO (OR DID) AT THE PLATE.

They may not admit it, or they may be like that friend with bad BO in high school who couldn't smell himself, but they have some idea that they're doing something original at the plate. When Youkilis or Counsell see clips of themselves, they must understand fans' fascination with their stances. I can't confidently say this of Mo Vaughn. I'm pretty sure Mo would be very surprised that he's on this list. He didn't squat down like Henderson, he didn't angle his bat like Tettleton or Franco. He didn't sit down like Bagwell or Rowand. And he certainly didn't wave his bat like Sheffield. So why did he make the list?

Let's dissect.

How he ever hit 99-mile-per-hour fastballs is beyond me. I know I've said this about other hitters, but it's extra true of Mo. Like a card player with an understanding of his terrible poker face, Mo always looked like he was trying to hide from the pitcher. His head was cocked almost parallel to the ground, like he's going to put it on a pillow and go to sleep, and his right arm and shoulder were like a veil over his face. Like a woman in Saudi Arabia, only the whites of Mo's eyes were visible as he peeked at the pitcher. Mo's face probably screamed that he couldn't hit a good curveball, but it took teams years to figure that out.

I can't catch an underhand lob from five feet away when I do what Mo did, let alone hit a 95 mph fastball.

His girth and gumption disabled his follow-through from completion. He would stick his swing up high and begin an entertaining run toward first all in one clunky motion. He really was the Big Papi of the mid-'90s Red Sox. Mo Vaughn was a great hitter whose light shined brightest in Beantown and quickly faded in Anaheim and New York. Thankfully, his stance lives forever in the hearts and minds of Red Sox Nation. Other than Youkilis, I'm not sure there's a Red Sox stance that gets as big a laugh from fans.

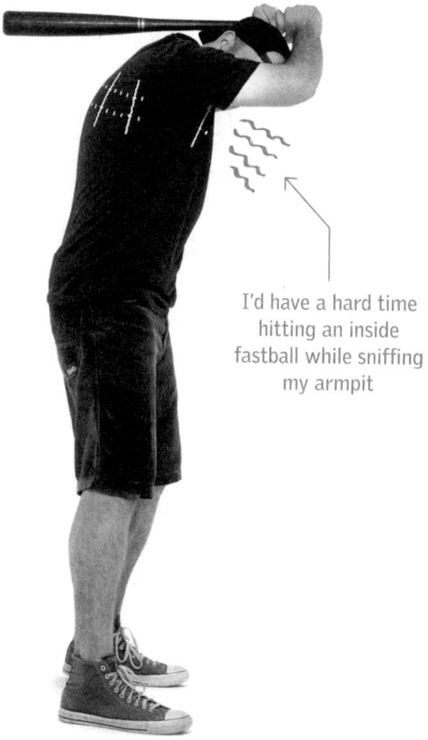
The "Headless Hitter"
I'd have a hard time hitting an inside fastball while sniffing my armpit

Special
SUGGESTED STANCE
Little tip: one way to get out of a hitting slump is to actually see the ball

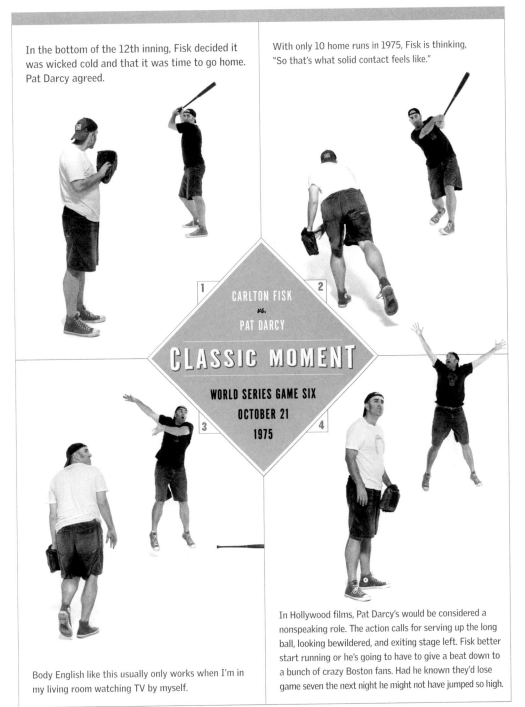

In the bottom of the 12th inning, Fisk decided it was wicked cold and that it was time to go home. Pat Darcy agreed.

With only 10 home runs in 1975, Fisk is thinking, "So that's what solid contact feels like."

CARLTON FISK

vs.

PAT DARCY

CLASSIC MOMENT

WORLD SERIES GAME SIX

OCTOBER 21

1975

1 2 3 4

Body English like this usually only works when I'm in my living room watching TV by myself.

In Hollywood films, Pat Darcy's would be considered a nonspeaking role. The action calls for serving up the long ball, looking bewildered, and exiting stage left. Fisk better start running or he's going to have to give a beat down to a bunch of crazy Boston fans. Had he known they'd lose game seven the next night he might not have jumped so high.

BATTING STANCE GUY
BEST OF THE REST

DAVE KINGMAN

OF-1B
METS
DAVE KINGMAN
TOPPS

DAVE KINGMAN WAS THE BARRY BONDS OF HIS ERA. HE STRUCK OUT MORE THAN BARRY DID, BUT WHEN HE HIT HOME RUNS, HE HIT BOMBS. HE ALSO ONCE SENT A DEAD RAT THROUGH THE MAIL TO A REPORTER. *GULP.*

Our neighbor's cat used to bite rats' faces off and leave them on their living room floor. Cat experts say that it's the cat's way of communicating affection. Hmmmmm. Thanks, kitty. This might be why I've never had a cat as a pet.

Kong doesn't get the same pass. For years he had the most home runs for a Hall-eligible non–Hall of Fame member. Now that distinction belongs to Mark McGwire. New Yorkers, Chicagoans, and Bay Area residents all know Dave Kingman. You didn't want to go to the bathroom and miss a towering homer by Kong. His feet were as wide apart as they could be, legs spread like he was really just trying to stretch his legs at the plate. Something tells me Von Hayes saw new possibilities from the left side of the plate when watching Kong bat as a kid.

Kong was surly and strong, but he ran the bases with his hands loose and close to his chest, making for a less than studly trot. Dave Kingman was close to being a movie character in my head. He was a villain, but what kind of villain was he? I remember attending games where friends would say, "OOOOOH yeah! Here comes Kingman!" and I'd look at his .222 batting average with the same home run count as Mike Davis and think, "What's the deal?"

He was like a stormtrooper. Whenever Luke or Obi Wan Kenobi talked about stormtroopers they made them sound like crazy, surgically precise killing machines. Offscreen, they always wiped out Jawa caravans and Ewoks with remarkable precision. On-screen was a whole different story. Look back at any *Star Wars* movie. Do they ever hit any of their targets? Their lasers never come close to hitting anyone of importance. They look like drunk robots who also might be blind. They graze Princess Leia in *Return of the Jedi*, but come on.

There, I said it. Dave Kingman was all flash—kind of like a way more talented and professional version of me. He hit a whole lot more home runs in the majors than I have, but he and I pay the same price for our Hall of Fame tickets.

Kong, you probably won't read this, but if you do, maybe you can just e-mail me a picture of a rat. My e-mail address is gar@battingstanceguy.com. Thanks.

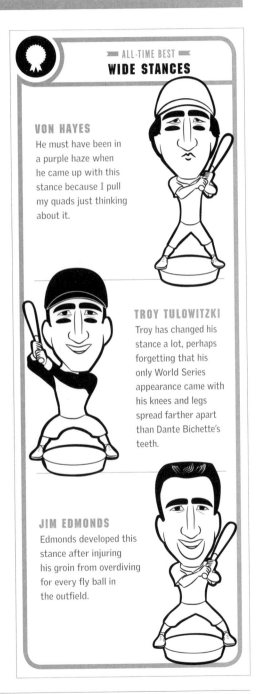

ALL-TIME BEST

WIDE STANCES

VON HAYES

He must have been in a purple haze when he came up with this stance because I pull my quads just thinking about it.

TROY TULOWITZKI

Troy has changed his stance a lot, perhaps forgetting that his only World Series appearance came with his knees and legs spread farther apart than Dante Bichette's teeth.

JIM EDMONDS

Edmonds developed this stance after injuring his groin from overdiving for every fly ball in the outfield.

normal
not normal

MY THOUGHTS ABOUT

THE NEW YORK METS and CITI FIELD / SHEA STADIUM

As the oldest of four kids, I've never been the little brother, the middle kid, or the baby. So I have no idea what the Mets, and Mets fans, go through every year. It must be tough having the Yankees as an older brother. They must be really sick of having their older brother be the mayor, the chief of police, and the movie star all in one. Joe Torre spent five seasons as the Mets manager and they never finished better than fifth in the division. He became the manager of the Yankees and he wins six pennants and four World Series rings. It's just not fair.

That's why 1986 was such a great year for Mets fans. The Yankees were in the midst of their worst 15-year span, and the Mets were beloved. They won 108 regular-season games and the World Series. When they knocked off the Yankees' bitter rival Red Sox, Mets fans even won a pat on the back from Bronx Bomber fans.

That 1986 team had such a great cast of characters. Because he'd played for the Expos, Gary Carter was my favorite catcher, and I watched that team closely. He helped lead that bizarre group of guys to the promised land. They snatched that victory with a mixture of the veteran savvy of Carter, Ray Knight, and Keith Hernandez and the cocky and spirited youth of Dwight Gooden, Lenny Dykstra, and Darryl Strawberry.

It's sad that everyone's strongest memory of that World Series victory is the Buckner moment, because those Mets were really good. It's telling that '86 is remembered as the Red Sox losing instead of the Mets winning. But let's face it: the Mets were the better team and were supposed to win. Sure, the Sox had a 23-year-old Roger Clemens, who won 24 games that year, and Wade Boggs hitting .357, but they also had "Oil Can" Boyd, Bob Stanley, and Calvin Schiraldi. Those guys just weren't winners. Watching Bob Stanley and his five-o'clock shadow take the mound was like watching your uncle who's a butcher about to have a heart attack at Thanksgiving dinner. Jesse Orosco may have been just as odd and scared-looking, but he was a way better pitcher. Wait, am I judging a bunch of professional athletes against my lone college intramural softball championship? Using words like winner and better when I'm sitting on my couch wishing I'd had a quarter of the career of guys like Stanley and Schiraldi is completely absurd.

The opening of Citi Field falls in line with everything else in Mets history. They open this amazing new field to replace forgettable Shea, and the Yankees open their fabulous new park at the exact same time. Let's see how that worked out for them. The Yankees sign every significant free agent, and they all live up to the hype; the Mets lose almost every significant star to injury. Yankee Stadium turns every warning track fly into a home run; new Shea turns every blast into a can of corn. The Yankees win it all and A-Rod finally gets his championship. The Mets finish 22 games below .500 and nobody cares. Go Mets!

Under-
developed
left field
Here's me with great hair
SHARP

citi FIELD
LET'S GO METS
Fully
developed
left field
Budweiser

Queens, New York / Citi Field and Shea Stadium: Citi Field has a slightly more developed left-field seating section than Shea. But in 1993 I had a slightly more developed head of hair.

BRET BOONE

BRET BOONE
second base SEATTLE MARINERS™

IN 1984 I WAS TAUGHT BY MY LITTLE LEAGUE COACH TO LINE UP MY MID-FINGER KNUCKLES WHILE GRIPPING THE BAT. I WAS TOLD THAT THIS WOULD ALLOW FOR THE BEST POSSIBLE SWING AND BAT ROTATION. BRET BOONE AND I WERE NOT IN THE SAME LITTLE LEAGUE.

His knuckles are lined up, however, on the complete other side of the bat. His wrists are lined up where my knuckles were. Couple that with his completely open squatting stance and we have ourselves some classic Mariners stance hilarity.

Let's talk about change. Barry Bonds's head got noticeably bigger in about 2000, Lenny Dykstra came to Phils' camp with 25 more pounds of muscle one year, and Mark McGwire hit 38 more home runs at age 34 than he did at 24. Things happen. People grow.

For years Boone was a nice second baseman who made many sliding catches and hit clutch doubles. Then one year on the Mariners he started going "Up-o Opp-o" (upper deck, opposite field—I first heard that term from Sean Casey, a man who never went Up-o Opp-o). Hmmm. Not even Jim Thome or Miguel Cabrera can do this with regularity. How does a second baseman start doing it? *Who cares*!?

I do. Because when he did it, he added my favorite bat dismount of all time to his repertoire. Bret Boone was a show. His run at MVP in 2001 was glorious. A victory for all imitators. He would swing so hard and finish with a countenance that said, "#@$%# STRAIGHT I just smacked one Up-o Opp-o!" And when the dust cleared, the opponents' second baseman had the bat at his feet. Boone also is the lone Top 50 member who gave us a Two-Strike Stance. He would throw caution to the wind for strikes one and two, but would hunker down for the two-strike pitch. Waaaay down. Still open, still arching his back backward while soloflexing his forearms toward each other. Bret Boone was awesome. I can't imitate noses, but Boone had a whole persona that reminded me of a Disney character. Part Seven Dwarfs, part swashbuckling *Pirates of the Caribbean.*

Bret Boone on the Reds, Padres, and Braves was like your college roommate who got married to a really nice girl right after graduation, had a couple of kids, loved dogs and coaching his kids' soccer team. Boone on the Mariners was that same roommate showing up at the 10-year class reunion with a 25-year-old blonde yoga instructor from New Mexico who loves to party. Dang, roomie, so lame of you to leave your family like that, but you don't make this book if you didn't make that change.

Bat as back-
scratcher

Sheffield is the only other righty I remember to do this with his leg and bat before swinging
Boone is right between Jim Edmonds and A-Rod for best season with frosted tips
Best bat release in baseball history
If he'd played in the '60s, something tells me Bob Gibson and Don Drysdale would have plunked him for this kind of tomfoolery

Yes, the bat
is on fire
↓

JIM LEYRITZ

Topps
TOPPS 2000
JIM LEYRITZ

THERE'S A 52.3 PERCENT CHANCE THAT JIM LEYRITZ HAD A TWIN BROTHER WHO PLAYED ALL OF HIS REGULAR-SEASON GAMES FOR HIM BECAUSE THE JIM LEYRITZ OF THE POSTSEASON WAS NOT THE SAME GUY.

He looked like regular-season Jim, with one of the more awkward and uncomfortable stances ever, but he only hit home runs and only hit them when it counted.

Regular-season Jim was a glorified utility player who hit only 90 home runs in his entire career (one every 28 at-bats). Postseason Jim hit homers every 7.6 at-bats and hit them at defining moments. I remember a rain-soaked walk-off homer in the Bronx Zoo in the 1995 ALDS against the Mariners to give the Yanks a 2–0 series lead (that they'd later squander). His game-tying three-run bomb off the Braves' Mark Wohlers in the 1996 World Series was his biggest moment as a Yankee, and arguably the kick start to the most recent Yankee dynasty and the death knell for the would-be Braves dynasty. The Yanks went on to win that game in 10 innings. He hit four home runs for the Padres in the 1998 postseason to catapult them to the World Series (where they got swept by the Yankees). Amazingly enough, Leyritz rejoined the Yankees in 1999, and in his only at-bat in that year's World Series against the Braves, hit a solo homer in the bottom of the eighth inning of game four. It's fitting for Leyritz's career that his last homer happened to be the last homer of the millennium.

Not since Super Joe McEwing has baseball seen a front leg so straight with a back knee so bent while keeping shoulders upright. Leyritz's arms would hitch while his knee mule-kicked like Matt Holliday's as the pitch was delivered. He really turned into a circus clown when he did the Mickey Rivers baton twirl after taking a pitch.

You take the stance, the bat twirl, his giant head, the mule kick, the hands hitch, his flair for the dramatic, and the fact that his voice was hoarser than Penn Jillette's, and I'd swear he was an infomercial for the pocket batting-stancer. Free shipping (he was traded at midseason in four consecutive years) and we'll throw in two top 10 finishes in hit by pitches for no extra charge!!!

ALL-TIME BEST
LEG KICK

MATT HOLLIDAY
Take away the bat and he's in a pitcher's wind-up motion. For some reason, this stance works only in the National League unless your name is Chris Stynes.

ORLANDO HERNANDEZ
Imitate Orlando's pitching motion in a backyard Wiffle Ball game and try not to knee yourself in the face.

BRONSON ARROYO
My chiropractor once told me I have the joints of an 80-year-old woman, which is why I'll never imitate Bronson and his Radio City Rockettes' leg kick.

High elbow →
← High elbow
paolo
Straight leg

Bat
wiggle
Leg kick
This swing
only works
in October
Toe tapping
to first base

PETE ROSE

NL
ALL STAR
3rd Base
PETE ROSE
REDS

ALL YOU NEED TO UNDERSTAND PETE ROSE IS TO SEE THE CLIP OF ROSE DRAWING A WALK AND THEN TAKING A PATH TO FIRST BASE THAT INVOLVED HIM CHUCKING HIS BAT, PUFFING OUT HIS CHEST, AND GLARING AT THE PITCHER LIKE HE'S GOING TO CHARGE THE MOUND.

Add a bowl cut his mother gave him that covered his ears so he looked like Nicholas Bradford on *Eight Is Enough* and you've got classic Rose. A walk? He wanted hits so badly he would taunt the pitcher for not throwing him a pitch he could hit. A walk's as good as a hit in most people's minds. Not Pete's. He and his full head of hair wanted hits, and only hits.

It wasn't until Rose's lifetime ban that I noticed the irony of my VHS copy of *Baseball: The Pete Rose Way*. All jokes aside, Pete really did play incredibly hard. He was a guy who wasn't afraid to get his uniform dirty.

Here's my open letter to Bud Selig:

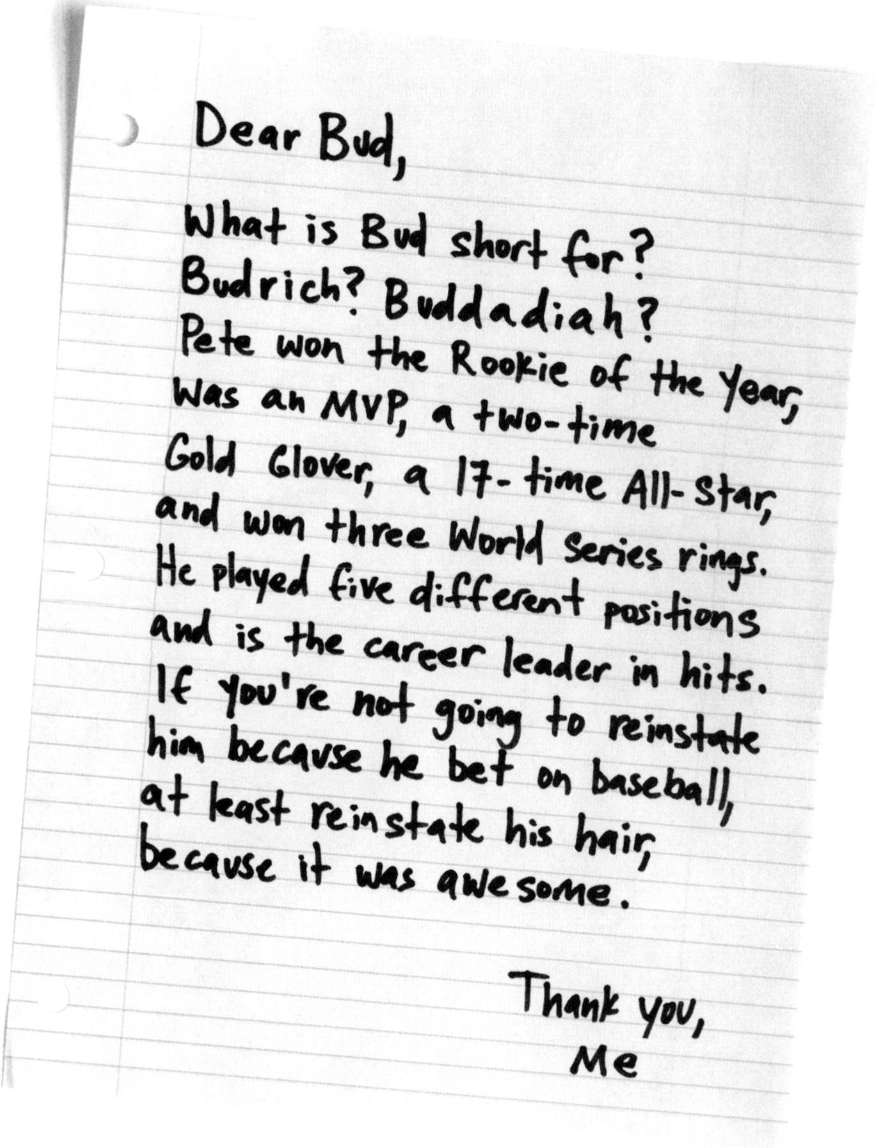

Dear Bud,

What is Bud short for?
Budrich? Buddadiah?
Pete won the Rookie of the Year,
was an MVP, a two-time
Gold Glover, a 17-time All-star,
and won three World series rings.
He played five different positions
and is the career leader in hits.
If you're not going to reinstate
him because he bet on baseball,
at least reinstate his hair,
because it was awesome.

Thank you,
Me

BIG RED
14
MACHINE

Best team nickname ever

On-deck-circle scowl

Looked the same lefty or righty

Second-best switch-hitter of all time?

MY THOUGHTS ABOUT

THE CINCINNATI REDS *and* THE GREAT AMERICAN BALL PARK

Most fans don't ever change team allegiances. Even if they move to a new city, wherever they first fell in love with baseball is where their heart lives. If they live in a new city for 20 or 30 years, they might start to pay attention to that new team, but it never feels the same. Expansion can mess with loyalty. People in Colorado, Florida, and Arizona who never really had hometown teams suddenly have a real team they can call their own. They get their first marriages annulled or divorce themselves from the teams of their youth. Braves fans in Florida found themselves with a new "home team" in their town and made the transition to the Rays or the Marlins. Nobody in Phoenix is actually from Phoenix, so every Diamondback fan switched from another team.

With all this said, I've met tons of Cincinnati Reds fans who have moved out of Ohio and set up shop in a big city and become a fan of that new team. Since the wire-to-wire first-place 1990 World Champs, the Reds have been on a stinky run of terrible finishes. Long-distance dating got rough for Reds fans. No spark. So when the Nationals move into town, you decide it's time to make a clean break. When you move to Boston and you're a baseball fan, you get infected because your immune system is weak.

The Reds haven't been lovably bad or tragically bad. They've just been boring losers. They've had some really great players who didn't make them winners. Ken Griffey Jr., Sean Casey, and Adam Dunn all played for the Reds but failed to get them to the postseason.

The 1970s Reds were a dynasty. Dubbed "the Big Red Machine," they had the best team nickname ever. They had such an amazing roster that when half the team went to Philly in 1983, the Phillies won the National League pennant and went to the World Series.

I am fond of a handful of terrible jersey and hat combos. The White Sox, Pirates, and Astros had some wonderfully hideous uniforms whose atrociousness should be celebrated. For some reason the 1995 Reds' hats are on the bad side of bad and quite possibly the worst of my lifetime. A white hat with red pinstripes just isn't a good look. No thanks. It looked like something I'd find in Jackson, Mississippi, at a closeout sporting goods store ridding the shelves of imitation-Starter gear. It doesn't matter to me that the '95 Reds made the playoffs; winning doesn't fix the problem. Current Reds uniforms aren't much better and seem to be bad in the same way that the team is bad—boring bad.

As a teenager, I had one opportunity to be a batboy during a major league game. My buddy Justin Speier, whose dad was playing for the Giants, called me with the news that a batboy couldn't make the Giants/Reds game at Candlestick that day. I was absolutely geeked at the prospect of being on the field during a real game. The bad news was that I had a Senior Minor Little League playoff game that day. "Dad, I can meet Eric Davis!!" My dad said, "Son, you made a commitment to your team. No." Another opportunity to be a batboy never emerged.

But maybe that lesson is the reason I managed to graduate from college, am still married to my wife, and can always be counted on to honor silly bets I've made over the years that usually involve ingesting things that make you sick. Thanks, Dad. Commitment and follow-through are important.

Cincinnati, Ohio / Great American Ball Park:
This was the last stop on a whirlwind 48 hours in Middle America in 2005. We'd seen a Yankees/Tigers game at Comerica on a Friday, visited the Rock 'n' Roll Hall of Fame in Cleveland on Saturday morning and the Pro Football Hall of Fame in Canton, Ohio, in the afternoon, a Marlins/Pirates game in Pittsburgh Saturday night, and finished it off with this Cardinals/Reds game in Cincinnati on Sunday afternoon.

JAY BUHNER

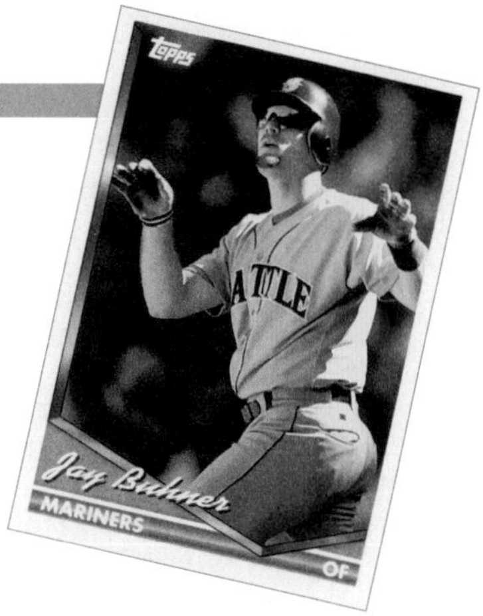
Topps
SEATTLE
Jay Buhner
MARINERS
OF

WHEN I WAS A SENIOR IN HIGH SCHOOL, RIDING THE PINE WITH THE VARSITY BASEBALL TEAM, THE GUY WHO STARTED OVER ME IN RIGHT FIELD WAS A SOPHOMORE—A TREMENDOUS ATHLETE NAMED DAMON BOWERS.

He would go on to play college and arena football, and he was just an all-around superior player. As soon as I saw him take the field I knew my days were numbered. I was Jay Buhner to Damon's Ichiro Suzuki. Buhner's time with the Mariners was done the moment seven-time batting champ Ichiro Suzuki landed Stateside. And when Bones was done, he was done. Too many wall crashes and too many nicks on his head from his Bic razor left him ready to hang it up after 14 seasons, and one great *Seinfeld* reference, with the Mariners.

Bones had one of the most menacing stances. He stood wide open, facing the pitcher with his bat hanging precariously high. His was a less flamboyant version of Tony Batista's stance. He'd hit the ball, and the bat would bounce off his shoulder like Shawon Dunston. Buhner hit more than 40 home runs in three consecutive seasons, but he was a career .254 hitter who struck out 175 times in 1997. Statistics are just numbers, but it does seem odd that despite being a Gold Glove right fielder, he stole only 6 bases in his entire 15-year career. He got caught stealing 24 times. To put it in perspective: Big Papi has stolen 10 bases and been caught only 5 times in his 13-year career. Bones had only 3 more stolen bases in his career than Doug Mirabelli, the only player in Red Sox history slower than Big Papi. How does that happen?

Bad to the "bones"
Batista-esque
Sweep the leg Johnny

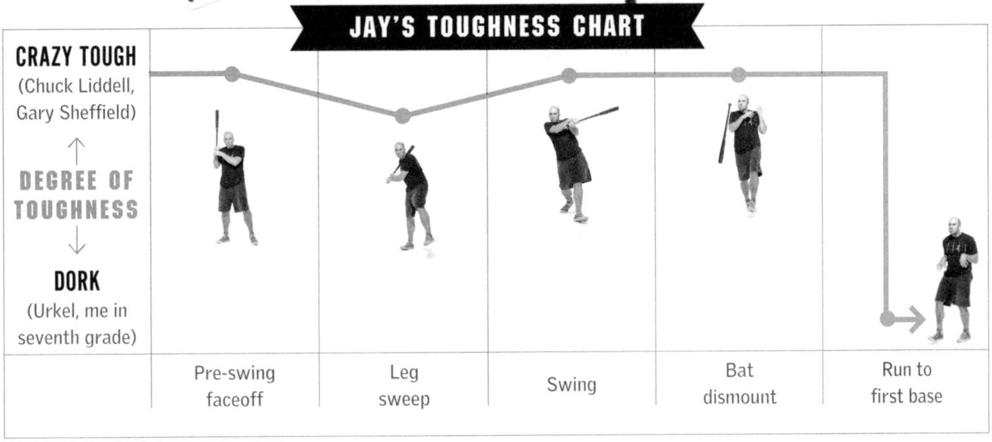
JAY'S TOUGHNESS CHART
CRAZY TOUGH
(Chuck Liddell, Gary Sheffield)
DEGREE OF TOUGHNESS
DORK
(Urkel, me in seventh grade)
Pre-swing faceoff
Leg sweep
Swing
Bat dismount
Run to first base

CARNEY LANSFORD

Topps
A's
OAKLAND ATHLETICS
3B
CARNEY LANSFORD

CARNEY LANSFORD'S STANCE WAS JUST THE PRECURSOR TO WHAT HE'S DONE SINCE RETIREMENT.

Lansford was the San Francisco Giants hitting coach until the end of the 2009 season. You could say that's like giving the inmates the keys to the asylum. Or you can say that Giants general manager Brian Sabean and manager Bruce Bochy should be applauded for the decision. I'm saddened by the fact that he's no longer the hitting coach. If there's one message I hope to spread it's that hiring Lansford for that job was brilliant. Pablo Sandoval? Eugenio Velez? Aaron Rowand, Randy Winn, and Freddy Sanchez? This might be the wackiest collection of stances in the league. To call Lansford a visionary might be an understatement. The 2009 Giants might not have made the playoffs despite having two of the best arms in baseball, but they sure were fun to watch at the plate. They may have been close to last in just about every offensive category in the National League, but they were first in my heart.

Having Lansford as a hitting coach is almost like hiring me, just with slightly less cowbell. If I were the hitting coach there'd be mandatory jazz and tap dance lessons, we'd watch Michael Jackson's "Thriller" on repeat instead of game tape, Deion Sanders's autobiography would be required clubhouse reading, and everyone would have to wear tuxedos under their uniforms.

Hunchback
of Oakland

Attempting
to wring the
bat's neck

MICKEY RIVERS

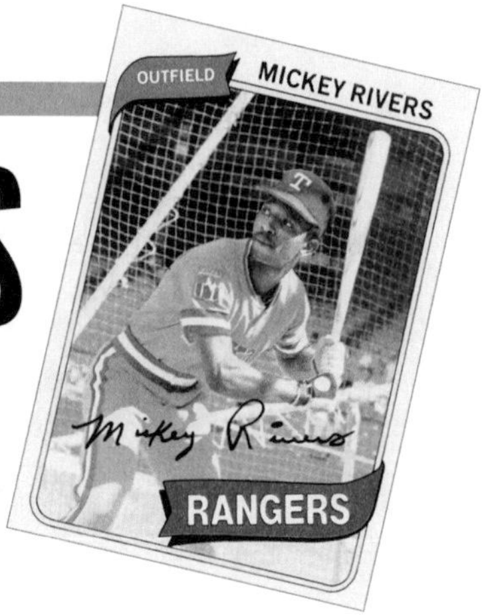
OUTFIELD
MICKEY RIVERS
RANGERS

PEOPLE LOVE MICKEY RIVERS.

IT MIGHT BE BECAUSE HE WAS A YANKEE, BUT THAT OFTEN CUTS BOTH WAYS.

It also might be because Mickey is like a non–Hall of Fame version of Rickey Henderson. Similar first names, both leadoff hitters, both threw lefty, both played outfield, both crouched incredibly low to the ground, and both made enormous splashes in the ALCS.

It might be because he won two World Series rings in his three and a half years with the Yankees. He was also an All-Star in 1976—a year in which he batted .312 and stole 43 bases. He also had a .308 average in his 29 postseason appearances, something that New York fans, like all good baseball fans, appreciate more than gaudy and meaningless regular-season statistics.

The real reason fans of the '70s love Mickey is that Mickey, like Rickey, referred to himself in wacky ways when he was quoted. He said ostentatious things, confusing things, things like "Me and George and Billy are two of a kind" and "pitching is 80 percent of the game and the other half is hitting and fielding" or "I don't get upset over things I can't control, because if I can't control them there's no use getting upset. And I don't get upset over the things I can control, because if I can control them there's no use in getting upset." It's hard to argue with that.

Mickey thrived in an age before free agency and massive corporate dollars, when players were oddball characters who spoke their minds, even if it made no sense. It seems that the only players willing to speak their minds in today's game are guys like Milton Bradley, who just seem angry. I'd appreciate Milton a whole lot more if he only referred to himself in the third person and blamed his poor play on plate tectonics or the phases of the moon. Or what if he was like the little kid in *The Shining* who talked with his finger and said stuff like "I'm sorry, Coach Lou, but Milton isn't here right now"? Now, wouldn't that be a whole lot more interesting? Or just weird. The problem with all this comes down to performance. It reminds me of something Crash Davis says in *Bull Durham*: "You'll never make it to the bigs with fungus on your shower shoes. Think classy, you'll be classy. If you win 20 in the show, you can let the fungus grow back and the press'll think you're colorful. Until you win 20 in the show, however, it means you are a slob."

Major bat wiggle
Him being pigeon-toed may explain his slightly awkward pimp strut from the on-deck circle

Rivers and Leyritz are the only two guys not in a high school marching band that I've ever seen do a baton twirl after taking a pitch

MY THOUGHTS ABOUT

THE TEXAS RANGERS and RANGERS BALLPARK IN ARLINGTON

When I visit my friend Barry Winford in Jackson, Mississippi, I like to ask him about his impressive college baseball team and his years in the minor leagues. He and his twin brother were on the fantastic Mississippi State teams of the mid-'80s with Rafael Palmeiro, Bobby Thigpen, and Will Clark. Barry once told me about spring training with the Rangers in 1990 when he hit a double and was greeted at second by Cal Ripken Jr., who said, "They call you Winnie, right?" These are amazing stories for a big kid like me to hear. If you ask, Barry will rattle off some of the guys in the minors at the same time as him. Names like Darren Oliver, Sammy Sosa, Robb Nen, Juan Gonzalez, and Ivan Rodriguez get dropped without hesitation. It's not until you think about it, and are reminded by Barry, that you realize all of these guys were actually Rangers to start their careers.

Look at the other players the Rangers have had over the years: Ivan Rodriguez, A-Rod, Michael Young, Ian Kinsler, Ruben Sierra, Al Oliver, Julio Franco, Nolan Ryan, Rusty Greer, Alfonso Soriano, Dean Palmer, Kenny Rogers, John Wetteland, Mickey Rivers, Josh Hamilton, and José Canseco. Add every one of these players up and you know what you get? One postseason win. Not one series win, one game. And that took Juan Gonzalez hitting two home runs in Yankee Stadium. Forty-nine years as a franchise and just one postseason win.

I'm not sure there's a more star-crossed team in baseball than the Rangers. Yes the Cubs, blah blah blah. I know the Red Sox took 86 years, the White Sox 88 years, the Indians a long time, I know, I know, I know. When you consider the fact that the Rays won the American League in 2008 and the Rockies won the National League in 2007, coupled with the three rings combined for the Marlins and the Diamondbacks, it's sad to realize how inconsequential the Rangers are. The Mariners even won the 1995, 2000, and 2001 ALDS.

How star-crossed is this franchise? They had the American League MVP and home-run champ in A-Rod for three last-place finishes. Ivan Rodriguez played MVP-quality ball with the Rangers but in his first season away from them he won the NLCS MVP and the World Series with the Marlins. Ouch. They didn't televise Nolan Ryan's seventh no-hitter. That's right. Anytime you see highlights of that game, it's the Blue Jays' telecast. Just incredible. They produced the only "header" home run in baseball history when the Indians' Dave Clark clubbed one off José Canseco's head for a ricochet dinger. Watch the full replay of that moment sometime. Center fielder David Hulse asked Canseco if it hit his head, while laughing, and Canseco shook his head, insisting that it hit his glove. No way, José. Incidentally, Hulse roomed with Barry Winford in the minors. Barry told me their wives went on the road with them. Living the dream! In the minors, rooming with other married couples. Baseball fever, catch it.

Rangers Ballpark in Arlington is a lovely place to catch a Rangers' loss. It might be the only stadium in the world where melting is a real possibility. The heat of north Texas is really something that should be avoided. I start sweating when I hear the word "Texas."

NIVERSIT
TENNESS
HATTANO

Arlington, Texas / Rangers Ballpark in Arlington: My buddy Jim Goodwin and I shared a passion for commemorative plastic cups, but we did not share my passion for ironic facial hair.

MARQUIS GRISSOM

Topps
Marquis Grissom
OF—ATLANTA BRAVES

MARQUIS GRISSOM IS THE STORY OF LINDSAY LOHAN, SCARLETT JOHANSSON, ALYSSA MILANO, AND NICOLE EGGERT.

As young girls, all four were adorable child actresses who starred in wholesome movies and television shows, always playing the big-name star's child. So as kids, they were all overshadowed by their costars. Scott Baio, Tony Danza, Robert Redford, and Jamie Lee Curtis were all bigger stars than Nicole, Alyssa, Scarlett, and Lindsay.

But that changed for each of these ladies when they grew up. Nicole left *Charles in Charge* to play Summer Quinn on *Baywatch*. Alyssa got some tattoos and started dating Major League Baseball players and guys like Justin Timberlake. Scarlett Johansson got lost in Tokyo with Bill Murray, appeared nude on the cover of *Vanity Fair*, and started dating guys like Justin Timberlake. Lindsay . . . Lindsay, Lindsay, Lindsay. I'm not sure she dated Justin, but other than that, she's probably done everything that the other ladies have done plus a bunch of other stuff not fit for print.

Grissom spent the first 10 years of his career as Josie Davis on *Charles in Charge*. A nice human being, totally adorable, standing straight up in his stance, knees slightly bent, lifting one leg up before he swung, with his hands in a normal spot. Wholesome and PG-rated, he really was Lindsay in *The Parent Trap*, covered in freckles and cute as a button.

During the twilight of his career with both the Dodgers and the Giants, Grissom went crazy. We're talking *Baywatch*, lower-back tattoos, *Maxim* magazine covers, and paparazzi outside his house. He held his bat higher than any Dodger ever has, and with the Giants he stuck the bat on his shoulder and downward while hopping on his feet.

Did Marquis's transformation have any impact on his stats? In 1993, for the Expos, he hit .298 with 19 home runs, 95 RBIs, and 27 doubles. Ten years later, with the Giants, he hit .300 with 20 home runs, 79 RBIs, and 33 doubles. Remarkably consistent. The big difference for Marquis in his career was on the basepaths. He stole 78 bases in 1992 but only 11 in 2003. I guess that's what living in the fast lane will do to you.

B.C. (BEFORE COMEDY)

Stance with THE EXPOS, BRAVES, INDIANS & BREWERS

First 2/3 of career, including hitting → safely in 15 straight World Series games

A.D. (AFTER DODGERS)

Stance with
THE DODGERS
← Unleashing his inner Counsell

Stance with
THE GIANTS
Bret Boone adjacent
Antsy jazz feet

MY THOUGHTS ABOUT

THE ATLANTA BRAVES *and* ATLANTA-FULTON COUNTY STADIUM / TURNER FIELD

Baseball has a problem with pitchers as league MVPs. Maybe it's because there's already the Cy Young Award for pitchers, and they feel like there isn't really the perfect award for a hitter unless they get the Triple Crown—something that seems impossible in the modern era. The National League really has a problem. The last pitcher to win an MVP in the National League was Bob Gibson, in 1968. The American League has shown pitchers a bit more love, but we're only talking five times since Denny McLain won it after going 31-6 with a 1.96 ERA for the Tigers in 1968.

I think baseball needs to rethink the MVP because what I've learned from the Atlanta Braves is that if you have at least three awesome pitchers, you'll always make the postseason. I know Chipper Jones, Terry Pendleton, Fred McGriff, and Andruw Jones all had great years for the Braves, but it's been pitching that's carried the Braves' torch into the postseason every year. If it wasn't for Tom Glavine, John Smoltz, Steve Avery, Greg Maddux, Kevin Millwood, and others, the Braves would have been decent-hitting teams that always finished in third place instead of making the playoffs for 14 straight seasons.

I know that the Kirk Gibson, Joe Carter, and Carlton Fisk home runs were mind-blowing and probably more "important" in the canon of postseason heroics, but the most dramatic single play in my lifetime was Francisco Cabrera's two-RBI single off Stan Belinda to end the 1992 NLCS. I sat with devout Pirate fan Ric Haupt in a dorm at Syracuse as we quietly watched Andy Van Slyke sit motionless in the outfield as the Braves mobbed Sid Bream at home plate. I'm not sure Ric cried himself to sleep that night, but his heart looked broken as he silently stood up after Bream's slide and disappeared. In a way, that moment was the death of a franchise. The Pirates haven't been close to competitive since.

I talked to Vinny Castilla recently about Cabrera's hit. He and Cabrera were the only two guys left on the bench for Bobby Cox to pinch-hit. Showing the depth of those Braves teams of the '90s, Castilla went on to become a Rockies legend.

Sean McDonough's call of that hit might be my favorite call of all time. You can tell that he just cannot believe it. McDonough sounded like me at 14 years old trying to talk to Melissa Couey—hoarse, excited, puberty-confused, nervous, shocked, and exhilarated. I think he lost his mind because it was so franchise-altering. There were two outs. Pirates were going to the World Series. My buddy Ric knew what that moment meant and so did Sean.

My buddy Baldwin Smith loves the Braves. He got married in Chattanooga, Tennessee, and after the rehearsal dinner 25 of his friends blindfolded him and made him hop a fence to sneak onto the Chattanooga Lookouts' field. Our plan was to give him a few words of advice and encouragement before he took the marriage plunge. My first bit of advice was that you shouldn't climb a fence blindfolded, but he'd already done that. For some reason, Baldwin started talking about the Sid Bream play, and we all decided to reenact the moment. A buddy in left as Bonds, other friends as the Pirates' infield, and Baldwin on second base as Bream. Fifteen guys got in the Braves' dugout, and on Cabrera's fake hit to left, Baldwin started running toward home plate in the pitch dark. Obviously, he's safe on a bang-bang play at the plate, where he's immediately dog-piled by the entire group. I took two lessons from that night. One, Braves fans love that moment in baseball history more than just about anything else, including their team actually winning the World Series. Two, a bloody leg sticks to tuxedo slacks.

Nilla

Atlanta, Georgia / Atlanta-Fulton County Stadium:
Little tip: you can save money on concessions by bringing your own Nilla Wafers and Combos to games. You can't tell from this picture, but it was blazing hot at Atlanta-Fulton County Stadium that day.

ERIC DAVIS

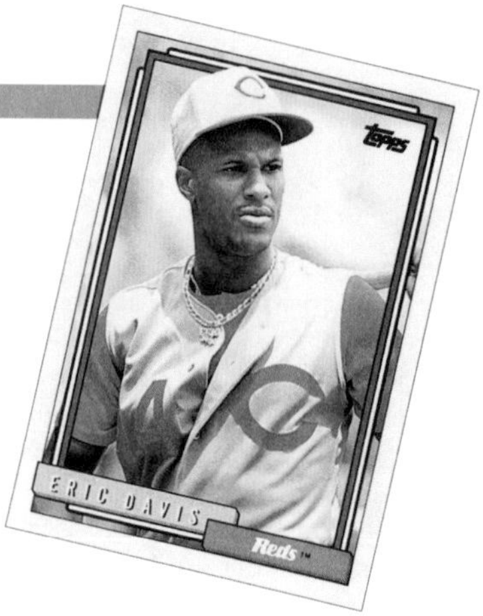
ERIC DAVIS
Reds

ERIC DAVIS
WAS AS LOOSE AS IT GETS.

In the 1990 World Series his bat was hanging so loose it looked like it was just going to fall out of his hands. He was an old-school version of Eugenio Velez, B. J. Upton, and Alexei Ramirez in that his power didn't mirror his size. He really had some amazing numbers in the late '80s. He hit 37 homers and stole 50 bases in 1987. And he did these in only 129 games. Often injured, he never played more than 135 games in a season. Indicative of his career, he missed the celebration after the Reds' 1990 World Series victory because he was in the hospital with a lacerated kidney after making a diving catch in left field. He also came back from colon cancer in 1998 and went on to have one of his best seasons as a pro, hitting .327 with 28 home runs.

Loose →

Not loose →

← Next time you watch a game, pay attention to what hitters bring the bat all the way back to the point of contact. Not many

BEN OGLIVIE

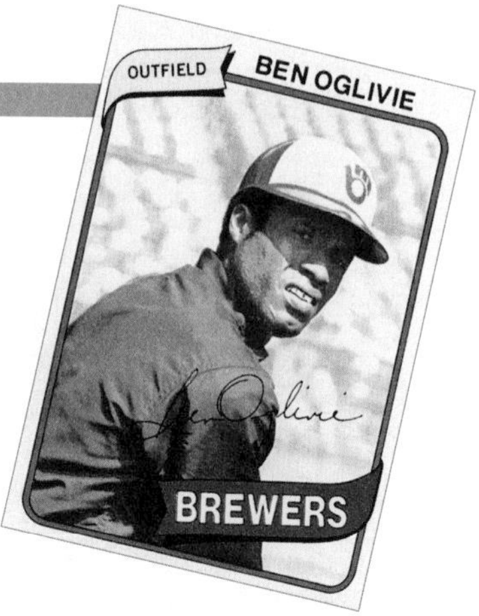

OUTFIELD
BEN OGLIVIE
BREWERS

BEN OGLIVIE WORE HIS PANTS UNUSUALLY HIGH.

Either the Brewers couldn't afford custom-made pants, or he was the first Urkel. Either way, he's probably never paid for a meal in Milwaukee, because that town still loves Harvey's Wallbangers. That 1982 Brewers team is still so beloved mainly because 2008 was the first time the Brewers made the playoffs since then.

Oglivie played in Japan, which suddenly makes him a whole lot more interesting. I'm pretty sure he got signed by the Kinetsu Buffaloes just because their scouts saw tape of his practice swing, which looked incredibly fast, like footage of Babe Ruth in the 1920s or like Benny Hill. He'd then bob up and down a few times before coiling a purposeful swing—at the actual pitch.

I love the Ben Oglivie routine. However, I've been asked only once to imitate Oglivie, and it was by Jim Gantner's daughter. I'm not sure if that even counts. The only reason she remembered Oglivie is that he played with her dad. As a person with a slightly less than healthy obsession with baseball, I'm always surprised by the regional aspect of baseball when it comes to certain levels of players and how or if they're remembered. If you're not from the Bay Area, you probably don't remember Shooty Babitt. If you're not from Boston, you probably never had Sam Horn on your fantasy baseball team. If you're not from the New York tristate area, you may have forgotten about Mackey Sasser's batting loops. That is, unless in ninth grade you did a paper like I did, titled, "Players Who Have Trouble Throwing Balls Whose Job Depends on It."

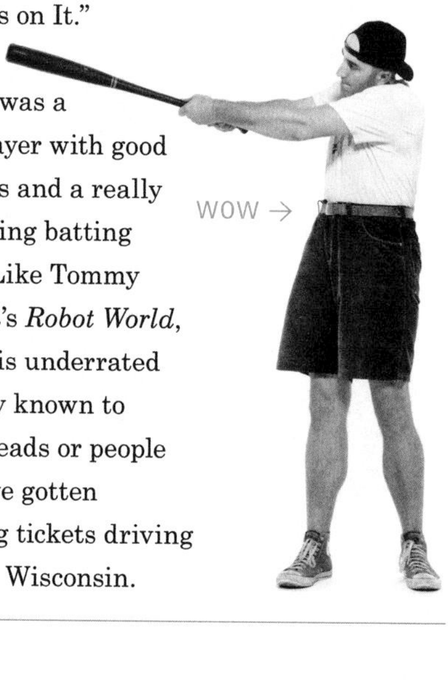

WOW →

Oglivie was a good player with good numbers and a really interesting batting ritual. Like Tommy Bartlett's *Robot World*, Oglivie is underrated and only known to cheeseheads or people who have gotten speeding tickets driving through Wisconsin.

MY THOUGHTS ABOUT

THE MILWAUKEE BREWERS *and* MILLER PARK

I love Milwaukee gimmicks. No major league franchise has created as many iconic and wholesomely hilarious moments to entertain fans. First, there is no cooler in-game entertainment than the Sausage Race. Five Brewers employees dress up in sausage costumes and sprint around a track while fans cheer on their favorite. My daughter's favorite is the chorizo, because she likes his sombrero. I'm not sure the ethnic stereotypes would work anywhere except Milwaukee, a place where innocence and homogeneity pervade. Does anyone know if the Polish sausage has ever won a race? I think someone should look into it.

The second most awesome Brewer gimmick is Bernie Brewer, the team's official mascot. After every Brewer home run, Bernie Brewer slides down a giant yellow slide. At old County Stadium, Bernie slid into a giant beer mug. Despite living in Miller Park, he now slides from his own personal dugout down to a platform above the left-field bleachers. I'm actually slightly saddened and surprised that political correctness has invaded Milwaukee in such an obvious way. I want the old-timey, retro feel of Miller Park to be intensified by the glorious celebration of public intoxication and gluttony. The team is called the Brewers, after all. The only thing better would be for North Carolina to have a team called the Smokies, with a mascot who takes a drag from a massive cigarette to celebrate a win or a home run. Because nothing says sports and victory quite like smoking.

Brewers players have brought their own gimmick to the game. On a walk-off hit or homer, or an otherwise emotional win, all the players immediately untuck their shirts. The best example was a Prince Fielder walk-off home run during the 2008 pennant drive. As the ball sailed over the wall and he rounded first base, Fielder untucked his enormous, tentlike jersey. He was then greeted at home plate by a mob of untucked teammates. I'm not sure what it means, but I have to believe that Ken Macha, the team's old-school manager, has to be driven crazy by such an absurd display of youthful enthusiasm. I'm waiting for the day when Ryan Braun hits a game-winning bomb in the bottom of the ninth and promptly takes off his pants.

The 1982 American League Cy Young Award winner was Pete Vuckovich and his mustache. He won 18 games for the Brewers that year, helping lead them to the World Series, where they lost to the Cardinals in seven games. Vuckovich was known for his odd behavior on the mound. He'd twitch and fidget, sometimes crossing his eyes and sticking out his tongue at opposing hitters. All that work should be viewed as a career-long audition for the role of a lifetime—that of Clu Haywood, the Yankee slugger and Rickey Vaughn nemesis in the movie *Major League*. I give the nod to Vuckovich for best actor over Ozzie Smith in *Rookie of the Year*, Carney Lansford in *Angels in the Outfield*, and Greg Ostertag in *Eddie*. Larry Bird was unforgettable in *Space Jam*, but he was really just playing himself, which doesn't count.

Milwaukee, Wisconsin / Miller Park:
I took this from the camera well on the first-base line while waiting to do the Brewers' postgame show. This was a packed house on a kids run-the-bases Sunday.

LENNY DYKSTRA

OF
LEN DYKSTRA

LENNY DYKSTRA SPORTED TWO DISTINCT STANCES IN HIS CAREER—ONE WITH THE METS AND ONE WITH THE PHILLIES.

With the Mets, he was closed, would squint his eyes and flutter his fingers while holding the bat in front of his body before the pitch. He would choke up slightly more than Pirates-era Barry Bonds and less than Mets-era Felix Millan.

By the time he reached the postseason with the Phillies, Dykstra had added a good 30 more pounds of muscle (cough). Bulked-up Dykstra found his arms setting up the swing farther back behind his body. He shut down the finger flutter but started to do a bouncing hitch right before the pitch was thrown. He looked like he was squatting like a catcher for a split second before he'd bounce right back into position. Add a massive chaw to his cheek and a slightly possessed look in his eye and you had a madman at the plate.

There are guys who step up when it counts and those who shrink under the pressure. A solid hitter and run scorer in the regular season, Dykstra was an absolute monster in the playoffs. During the regular season, in over 4,500 at-bats, Nails averaged a home run every 56 at-bats. In more than 100 post-season at-bats, he hit a home run every 11 at-bats. In the 1993 World Series against the Blue Jays, Nails hit .348 with 4 home runs and 8 RBIs in 6 games. He was a career .285 hitter who hit only 10 or more home runs twice in a regular season but who hit 10 home runs in just 112 postseason at-bats.

What I love about sports and baseball in particular is that guys like this exist. For every Bobby Bonilla and Vince Coleman, whose postseason numbers pale in comparison to their gaudy regular-season numbers, there are guys like Dykstra and Jim Leyritz who defied logic and scouting and all other rational thought when the lights were shining brightest.

@*ϟ◎!!
ϟ∂⊗*!!

Needless to say, my mom wasn't thrilled to discover, until after she bought it for me, that Lenny's 1987 autobiography *Nails* was littered with F-bombs

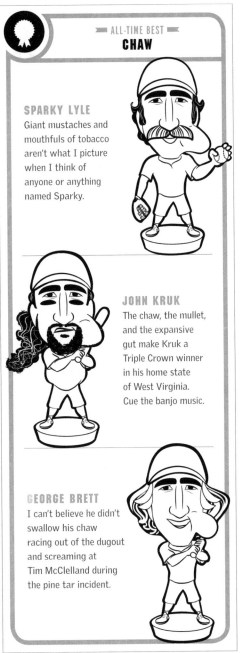

ALL-TIME BEST

CHAW

SPARKY LYLE
Giant mustaches and mouthfuls of tobacco aren't what I picture when I think of anyone or anything named Sparky.

JOHN KRUK
The chaw, the mullet, and the expansive gut make Kruk a Triple Crown winner in his home state of West Virginia. Cue the banjo music.

GEORGE BRETT
I can't believe he didn't swallow his chaw racing out of the dugout and screaming at Tim McClelland during the pine tar incident.

TONY EUSEBIO

Topps
Tony Eusebio
C — HOUSTON ASTROS

OF ALL PEOPLE IN THIS BOOK, TONY EUSEBIO MIGHT BE THE MOST SURPRISED TO FIND OUT HE IS MENTIONED.

I didn't grow up in Houston in the '90s, so the fact that I even know he played baseball is astonishing. I'm not trying to brag about my vast baseball knowledge, it's just that his career was really unremarkable. He has the fewest at-bats of any player in this book—over 100 fewer than Phil Plantier. And Plantier played for the Red Sox, so he gets automatic points for playing on a team with slightly crazy fans who take their team loyalty to the grave regardless of where they actually live. Eusebio played for the Astros for most of the '90s, which is a lot like playing for the Nationals now. They made the postseason a few times but were generally second fiddle to Smoltz and the Braves.

Picture a two-year-old drinking tons of water right before going to bed, then putting on a diaper and going to sleep. When that child walks out of his room in the morning, that's what Eusebio's stance looked like. It sagged. A lot. His shoulders slumped like your great-grandpa's, and his arms hung out over the plate as if he wanted to hold the bat up but had just finished a tough workout and didn't have the strength to lifts his arms that high.

I can't confirm this because photographic evidence of Eusebio at the plate doesn't exist, but I'm pretty certain that he fell asleep at the plate. Only opposing catchers and umpires would know for sure, because they would have heard him snoring.

All you need to know about Eusebio's place in Astros history is summed up by the fact that for a time he held the franchise record with a 24-game hitting streak. That was over a 45-game period. Classic.

ZZZZZZZZZZZZZZ

COCO CRISP

Coco Crisp.
ALLEN & GINTER'S
BROOKLYN. 2007 NEW YORK.

FIVE REASONS WHY COCO IS IN THIS BOOK:

1. HIS NAME. It's Coco Crisp. Maybe only Froot Loop or Cap'n Crunch would be more amazing. If my mom named me whatever cereal she was eating the morning of my birth it would have been Count Chocula. I could have been CC Ryness. That would have been way better than George Allison Ryness. On the Indians, Coco played in the outfield with Milton Bradley. Too bad Jody Gerut wasn't named Lexus Nintendo because that would have been awesome.

2. HE THRUSTS HIS HANDS toward the pitcher while bending his back knee and pointing his front leg unusually straight.

3. PUBLIC DISPLAY OF AFFECTION. His chin and his shoulder need to get a room as they make out with each other while he awaits a pitch. It's very distracting.

4. FLUTTERING TOP HAND. As the pitcher is about to release the ball, Coco's hand is fluttering on the bat like a moth on a lightbulb.

5. HE'S HONEST TO A FAULT. If you drive too fast on the freeway, you don't call the police to tell them to pull you over, do you? Crisp is one of a small handful of players who will occasionally check his own checked swing, pointing down to the base umpire to make the strike call. Uh, Coco (and Adrian Beltre), if the home plate umpire doesn't call it a strike, then the *only* outcome that can happen from you soliciting the base umpire to get involved is a bad one. Why bring him into the argument? He can only add a new strike call. It's mind-blowing, hilarious, and the number 5 reason Coco makes the list.

← Making his own chin music

When I met her, Adrian Gonzalez's wife asked me to imitate one player: Coco Crisp

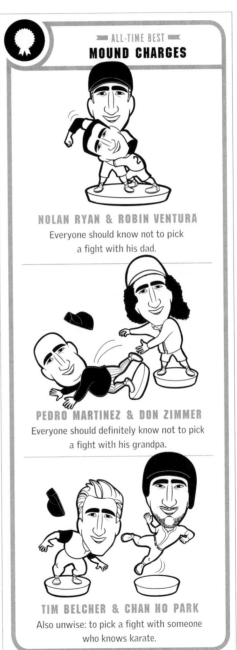

ALL-TIME BEST

MOUND CHARGES

NOLAN RYAN & ROBIN VENTURA

Everyone should know not to pick a fight with his dad.

PEDRO MARTINEZ & DON ZIMMER

Everyone should definitely know not to pick a fight with his grandpa.

TIM BELCHER & CHAN HO PARK

Also unwise: to pick a fight with someone who knows karate.

DON BAYLOR

DH-OF
ANGELS
DON
BAYLOR
TOPPS

WHEN MY CHILDHOOD FRIEND JUSTIN SPEIER MADE IT TO THE BIG LEAGUES AS A MEMBER OF THE BRAVES, I MET HIM IN THE LOBBY OF A LOS ANGELES HOTEL WHEN HE WAS IN TOWN ON A ROAD TRIP.

I remember it really clearly because he got his first base hit that night, which is funny because he's a relief pitcher. Standing in the lobby, we watched pillars of the Braves walk past us—Chipper Jones, Andruw Jones, Ryan Klesko, Greg Maddux, John Smoltz, Tom Glavine, and others. But it was hitting coach Don Baylor walking through the lobby that got my blood pumping. I turned to Justin and said something really smart like, "No way, Don Baylor."

Baylor was the embodiment of a tough veteran player when I was a kid. When I was in junior high and high school and he was in his late 30s, he was a World Series mercenary. He hit 31 home runs as the DH for the '86 Red Sox. In '87 he hit a huge home run off John Tudor in the World Series to help the Twins oust the Cardinals. If that wasn't enough, he fantastically DH'd for the A's the following year when they made it to the World Series. Three years, three different teams, and three straight World Series. Sure, Yogi Berra appeared in 14 World Series and won 10 rings, but they were all with the Yankees. Somehow, Baylor's achievement seems so much more unlikely, especially since it was with oddball teams that never looked like they had a chance to make it that far. Baylor held the modern record for getting hit by a pitch until he was recently surpassed by Craig Biggio. I think there's a really good chance that Baylor's antics at the plate had something to do with him getting plunked by opposing pitchers. As with many of the players in this book, Baylor was a league leader or close to it in this category for much of his career. He stood straight up, right over the plate, wiggled his bat, flexed his bicep like he was about to take two for flinching, and was shaking his whole body in anticipation of taking the punches. In this case, the punches were baseballs and Baylor seemed to love it.

THE 267 PLACES BAYLOR HAS BEEN HIT

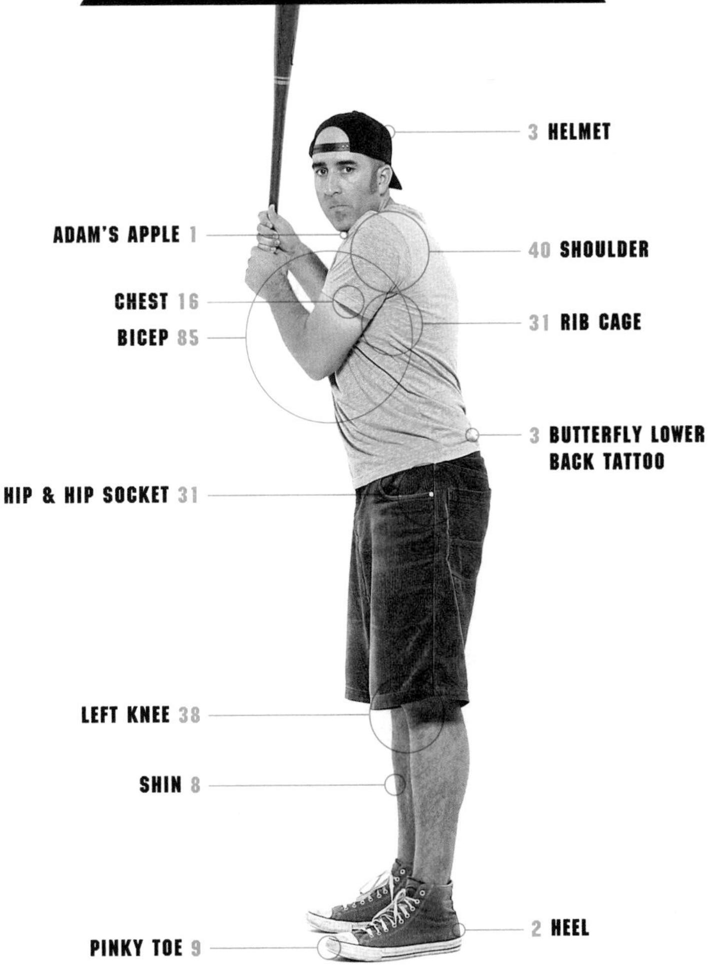
3 HELMET
ADAM'S APPLE 1
40 SHOULDER
CHEST 16
BICEP 85
31 RIB CAGE
3 BUTTERFLY LOWER BACK TATTOO
HIP & HIP SOCKET 31
LEFT KNEE 38
SHIN 8
2 HEEL
PINKY TOE 9

RYAN HOWARD

ryan howard
HERITAGE
PHILADELPHIA PHILLIES®
FIRST BASE

IF YOU TOLD ANY PLAYER WITHIN THE FIRST FIVE YEARS OF THEIR CAREER THAT THEY WERE GOING TO WIN ROOKIE OF THE YEAR, AN MVP, THE HOME-RUN TITLE, THE RBI TITLE, AND A WORLD SERIES RING, THEY'D TAKE IT.

Howard has done everything you can possibly do in your first five years, including striking out almost 200 times a year. Seriously, he's averaging 195 strikeouts a year in his career. Howard is the polar opposite of Rod Carew, and it's awesome to watch. There are dozens of players that do the samurai, but nobody gets their back hand (the left hand in Howard's case) as involved as Howard. Yes, Ichiro tugs his sleeve, but Howard takes it to a whole new level by pointing the head of the bat right at the pitcher while crouching and placing his left-hand fingers wide open while resting his left arm in an invisible sling. It's like a handicapped jazz hand, something Elvis probably did onstage circa 1967. When Howard steps and delivers a knockout swing, he'll show that it's gone by shaking his head and shoulders, throwing the bat to the ground in confident disgust, and speedwalking around the bases like the 55-year-old woman in your neighborhood at 6:00 A.M. Or like Lloyd McClendon after arguing and picking up second base before speedwalking off the field.

BASEBALL
FEVER
75%
Samurai
+
25%
Elvis
=
110%
Awesome

PIMP ROBOT STRUT TO FIRST BASE

ALL-TIME BEST

HOME RUN TROT

DAVE PARKER

If Major League Baseball had the NFL's rule book, I'm pretty sure Cobra would have been flagged for excessive end zone celebration.

PRINCE FIELDER

Fielder looks like me at my seventh-grade formal when I got stuck wearing my dad's dress shirt. I always wonder if he'll slow-dance with Alysha Lujan when he gets to home plate.

SAMMY SOSA

Hopping up and down doesn't help you get to first base any faster, but with 609 home runs, Sammy liked his chances of going yard and not getting thrown out at first. He might as well have Ozzie Smith backflipped to first base.

MY THOUGHTS ABOUT

THE PHILADELPHIA PHILLIES and CITIZENS BANK PARK

Philadelphia, Pennsylvania / Veterans Stadium:
Why drag the infield when you can vacuum it?

Philadelphia really has great sports fans. Yes, the Yankees and the Red Sox have passionate fans and the Cardinals and the Cubs have thoughtful, caring fans, but Philly is right at the top. The Phillies are the only pro sports franchise with 10,000 losses (Washington Generals notwithstanding), yet still they have a fanatical following. Phillies teams have been good very infrequently. Sure, they're good now with Howard and Werth and Victorino and were good in the late '70s and early '80s and for five minutes in 1993, but when they've been bad, they've been really bad.

And it's made fans from Philly really tough. They booed Santa Claus. They booed Mike Schmidt, the greatest third baseman of all time. During the 1993 NLCS, the Braves fans continued to do the tomahawk chop cheer in Atlanta. When asked how that cheer would work in Philly, closer Mitch Williams said Philly fans would throw real tomahawks. He wasn't exactly kidding.

Just think of the female fans of a given team. Cubs and Brewers girls want to have a beer and some fun and then get back in the car to listen to the Steve Miller Band. Dodgers girls are driving in after the top of the second inning and out in the bottom of the eighth inning. Angels girls TiVo *The Hills*, so they can stay for the entire game and look beautiful. Cardinals girls sit with their dad, who is scoring the game (4-6-3 double play, no RBI). Philly girls think Cole Hamels is dreamy and will smack you in the face if you say his 3-2 changeup could be better.

It's not that unusual for fans and players to look like each other. The 1993 Phillies really mirrored their crowd. With John Kruk, Lenny Dykstra, and Mitch Williams, the chaw and mullet factor was incredibly high. And I swear if you could have pulled half the dudes wearing Eagles Starter jackets out of the bleachers and lined them up next to Pete Incaviglia in left field, you would not have been able to tell who the player was.

Old Veterans Stadium was as rough as the fans. It was a massive, cookie-cutter stadium that really made no sense as a baseball stadium. The 700 level, where the really crazy and passionate fans roamed, was so high and so far from the field that you needed binoculars to really see anything. For a long time, the field was covered with a really bad AstroTurf that routinely blew out knees and ruptured tendons. Fortunately, Citizens Bank Park opened in 2004, and Philly fans and players finally got a stadium they deserved. I'm not sure having such a fancy field has changed the mentality of the fans, but it sure looks like it's helped the team win more games.

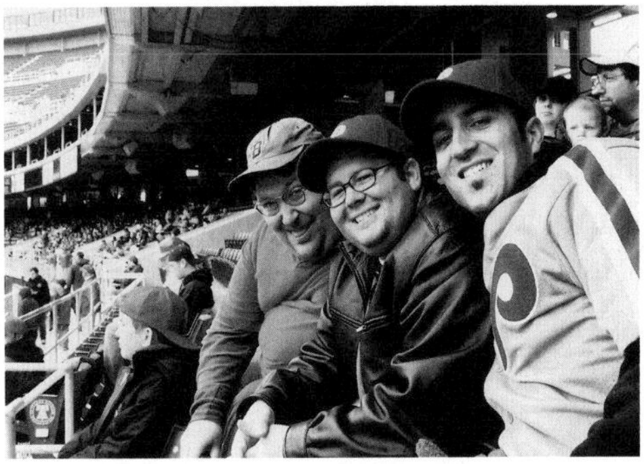

This was on my birthday in 2003, the last year the Phillies played at the Vet. My buddy Kern-Dog, who is from Philly, took me, my buddy Justin, my dad, and my brother to Pat's for cheese steaks before the game. Kerny and I saw Barry Bonds hit number 713 (one shy of Ruth's career total) in Citizens Bank Park three years later.

TONY PHILLIPS

A's
TONY PHILLIPS

TONY PHILLIPS IS ONE OF THE FEW PLAYERS IN MLB HISTORY TO BE INVOLVED IN THE FINAL PLAY OF TWO WORLD SERIES.

He struck out off Orel Hershiser to end the 1988 World Series. Then the very next year he fielded a carom off Mark McGwire's glove and flipped it to Dennis Eckersley to get San Francisco's Brett Butler at first to complete the 1989 World Series.

And just when you thought it would never happen again, it happened three years later with Joe Carter. Carter caught Mike Timlin's throw to first base after an Otis Nixon bunt attempt in 1992 and then followed up a year later with a Series-ending walk-off homer off Mitch Williams. Edgar Renteria also ended two World Series with his bat, getting a single off Charles Nagy in 1997 and grounding back to Keith Foulke in 2004 to give the Red Sox their first championship in 87 years.

What does all this have to do with anything? I have no idea, but it seems somehow appropriate that Tony Phillips, a switch-hitter, had the same swing lefty and righty. He moved his hands a ton while the ball was in the air, he kicked his front foot up as high as he wanted, he smiled huge, and he threw wild temper tantrums. He did what we all wanted to do but he got away with it.

← Breathing through his teeth
Flashiest leg kick by a utility player

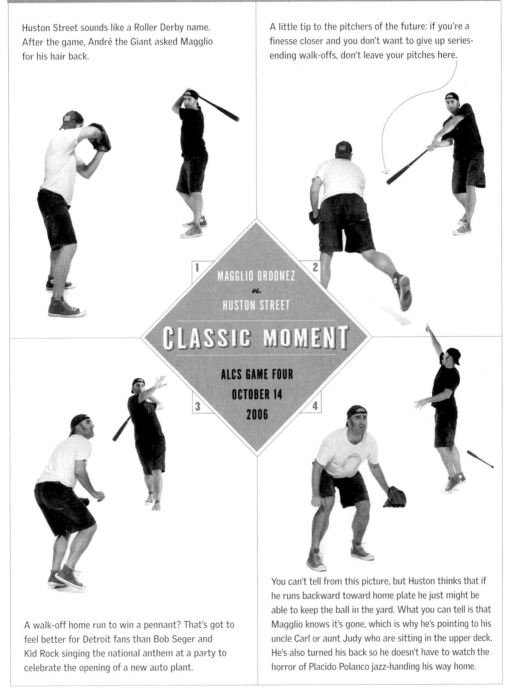

Huston Street sounds like a Roller Derby name. After the game, André the Giant asked Magglio for his hair back.

A little tip to the pitchers of the future: if you're a finesse closer and you don't want to give up series-ending walk-offs, don't leave your pitches here.

1 2 3 4

MAGGLIO ORDONEZ

vs.

HUSTON STREET

CLASSIC MOMENT

ALCS GAME FOUR

OCTOBER 14

2006

A walk-off home run to win a pennant? That's got to feel better for Detroit fans than Bob Seger and Kid Rock singing the national anthem at a party to celebrate the opening of a new auto plant.

You can't tell from this picture, but Huston thinks that if he runs backward toward home plate he just might be able to keep the ball in the yard. What you can tell is that Magglio knows it's gone, which is why he's pointing to his uncle Carl or aunt Judy who are sitting in the upper deck. He's also turned his back so he doesn't have to watch the horror of Placido Polanco jazz-handing his way home.

DISCO DAN FORD

Twins
DAN FORD
OUTFIELD
TWINS

THERE ARE PLAYERS WHO HAD CLOSED STANCES AND PLAYERS WITH CLOSED SHOULDERS, BUT NOBODY DID BOTH LIKE DISCO DAN FORD.

There has to be some terrible experience that I just missed where he got plunked in the face or the crotch, because he looked terrified of getting hit anywhere but his back. All he showed to the pitcher was his back and his uncool Glenn Wilson sunglasses. He had a couple of fairly good seasons over his 11-year career despite having a stance that ranks as one of the toughest to imitate and hit the ball out of the front yard while playing Wiffle Ball. I'm not sure where he got the nickname, but if you leave off the "Disco," he loses his identity. His real name is Darnell, and I'm guessing that he got the nickname for the work he put in off the field and not because he led the American League in sacrifice flies in 1979.

Disco is on a surprisingly odd list of hitters who hit three home runs in a single game. He never hit more than 21 homers in a season, but he's on a list with a bunch of big hitters like Sammy Sosa, Dave Kingman, Joe Carter, Mark McGwire, and A-Rod. What's possibly weirder is that Jeff Treadway, Von Hayes, Randy Milligan, Gerónimo Berroa, Willie Greene, and Hee-Seop Choi also are on that list. For every All-Star and

Hall of Famer on the list, there are 10 guys I barely remember. Chris Woodward? He's hit 33 home runs in a 10-year career, so the fact that he hit three in one game against the Mariners in the summer of 2002 makes almost no sense. On the long list of things that make baseball great, little details like this are right at the top. The fact that for one day, three shining moments, a guy like Chris Woodward burned brighter than anyone else on the field, is really special. That's the kind of thing that puts the Disco in Disco Dan Ford.

Disco: Smooth
Dan Ford: Not smooth

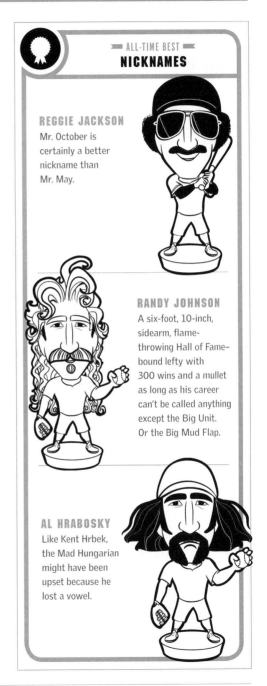

ALL-TIME BEST
NICKNAMES

REGGIE JACKSON
Mr. October is certainly a better nickname than Mr. May.

RANDY JOHNSON
A six-foot, 10-inch, sidearm, flame-throwing Hall of Fame–bound lefty with 300 wins and a mullet as long as his career can't be called anything except the Big Unit. Or the Big Mud Flap.

AL HRABOSKY
Like Kent Hrbek, the Mad Hungarian might have been upset because he lost a vowel.

JOE MORGAN

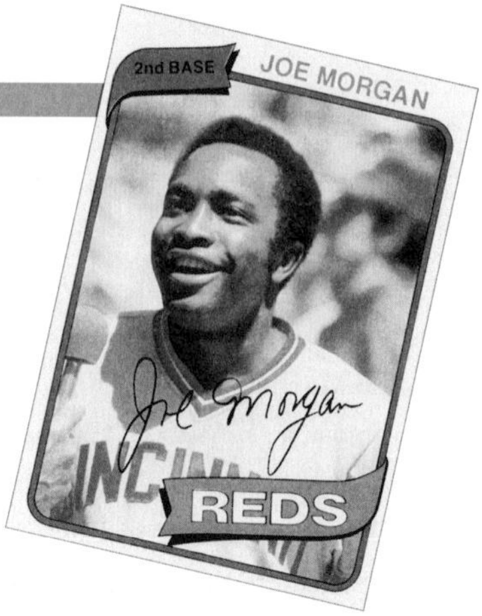
2nd BASE
JOE MORGAN
Joe Morgan
REDS

IF YOU'RE 35 YEARS OLD OR YOUNGER AND NOT AN OLD MOVIE BUFF, YOU PROBABLY THINK THAT JAMES GARNER WAS JUST A SPOKESMAN FOR MAZDA AND THE OLD DUDE IN *THE NOTEBOOK*.

And if you're that same age and a casual baseball fan, then you undoubtedly think that Joe Morgan is just the veteran color commentator for ESPN baseball who must have been an okay player because color commentators usually played the game.

I had to watch *The Great Escape* to realize that James Garner was once part of a dynamic duo with Steve McQueen. You also have to go back a little bit to know that Joe Morgan was one of the best second basemen in baseball history. At five feet, seven inches, Joe won the National League MVP in 1975 and 1976 and was a linchpin of "the Big Red Machine," the Reds dynasty that dominated the National League in the early and mid-1970s. The Machine featured Hall of Famers Pete Rose, Johnny Bench, and Tony Perez, so for Morgan to stand out on that team is exceptional. He was a 10-time All-Star and two-time World Champion who did everything well. He was a great fielder, got on base like crazy, stole a ton of bases, and hit for decent power. He also was consistently among the league leaders in sideburns. His muttonchops were a sight to behold.

Morgan is one of the most requested imitations for all fans over age 40 because he was one of the iconic players of the '70s but also because his stance was pure comedy.

His back arm flap while awaiting the pitch made him his day's Nomar Garciaparra. It looked like the catcher had just asked him to imitate a chicken flapping its wings. But what else would you expect from a dude who played for the Houston Colt .45s? That chicken wing's hit knocked in the game-winning run in game seven of the 1975 World Series, extending Red Sox fans' heartache for another 29 years.

Bat windup
MACHINE

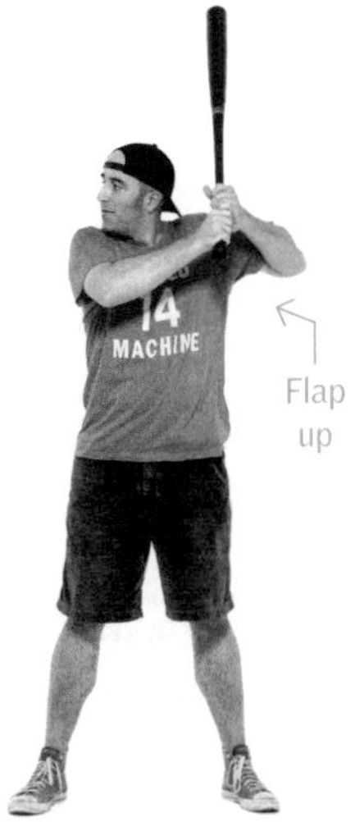
14
MACHINE
Flap up

14
MACHINE
Flap down

ALBERT PUJOLS

albert pujols
HERITAGE
ST. LOUIS CARDINALS
FIRST BASE

IF YOU'RE A FAN, PUJOLS IS EXACTLY WHAT YOU WANT IN A SUPERSTAR.

In the era of the team carousel, he's played for one team. Hammering the ball every season, he's put together the greatest start to a career since Lou Gehrig. He was the National League Rookie of the Year in 2001 and is also a three-time MVP. He's a guy who has Triple Crown numbers, batting for a high average with a ton of homers and RBIs. He's gregarious, all big smiles and laughter. During my on-field interactions with the Cardinals before a game, Pujols was missing from the team circle because he was shaking hands and kissing babies in the stands, as if stumping for votes.

And his batting stance does not disappoint. He gets really low to the ground to start his stance and then bobs up and down while scrunching up the left side of his face. He adds a left-eye squint, and suddenly he looks strangely like Popeye. It gets even better when he gets to two strikes, because he sticks his tongue out to the left side of his cheek. He really looks like a four-year-old trying to be a pirate.

After he crushes the ball, he launches the bat with his left hand toward the first-base dugout. Alex Rodriguez recently adopted this same bat toss. Both have a way of making the bat look like it weighs nothing. This toss and Gary Sheffield's pre-swing bat waggle are the top two reasons why, when I imitate players, I do it with a plastic bat.

Pre-stance crouch
I'd keep both eyes open and my tongue in my mouth, but I haven't won three MVPs

If you went to get a hot dog, you just missed me going yard
I think I just hit Big Mac land

1

Phat Albert could be the Cards' final out of the season. But when there is a Lidge, there is a way.

2

Albert is wondering if everyone gets free chalupas if he hits this one over the train tracks in left field. This wouldn't be the last time Lidge wishes he could have the pitch back.

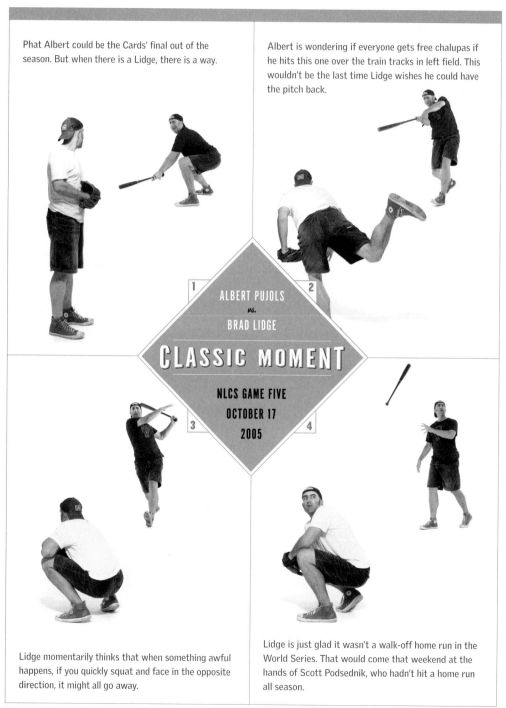

ALBERT PUJOLS

vs.

BRAD LIDGE

CLASSIC MOMENT

NLCS GAME FIVE

OCTOBER 17

2005

3

Lidge momentarily thinks that when something awful happens, if you quickly squat and face in the opposite direction, it might all go away.

4

Lidge is just glad it wasn't a walk-off home run in the World Series. That would come that weekend at the hands of Scott Podsednik, who hadn't hit a home run all season.

MY THOUGHTS ABOUT

THE ST. LOUIS CARDINALS and OLD/NEW BUSCH STADIUM

Despite having won the most World Championships in the National League and being second to only the Yankees in MLB history, the Cardinals don't make good villains. For some reason, nobody hates the Cardinals in the same way that people love to hate the Yankees and maybe the recently successful Red Sox. Even Cubs fans would go grab a beer with a Cards fan after a hard-fought game. The Cardinals are the equivalent of actress Kate Winslet. She is pretty, owns a fussy English accent, starred in the second biggest movie of all time, and constantly gets offered the best movie roles. But somehow, no one hates Kate Winslet. She wins, but we don't feel threatened by her. Angelina Jolie, on the other hand, makes our wives nervous and a little angry. I guess you can be too pretty.

The thing is that Cardinal fans are the laid-back version of Yankee and Red Sox fans. That is, really knowledgeable about the game but slightly less crazy. They cheer for a no-outs groundout that gets the runner over to third because they know a sacrifice fly scores the runner, but they're less likely than a Sox or Yankee fan to get into a fight in the stands if the runner doesn't score. This is surprising, since the Cardinals do play in new Busch Stadium, a place where alcohol consumption is obviously encouraged.

Like the team, old Busch Stadium, despite being terrible, never drew the ire of other fans and somehow got a pass on being included on the worst cookie-cutter stadium with horrible AstroTurf list. It might be because the stadium fit the team. My strongest memory of the Cards is the 1987 team. Manager Whitey Herzog almost won that year's championship with smoke and mirrors. They were one of the last teams to use good pitching, that enormous park, stolen bases, bunts, more stolen bases, and Tom Lawless to win ball games.

They went to game seven of the World Series with Curt Ford, Jim Lindeman, José Oquendo, and Dan Driessen (unless you're from St. Louis and were 12 years old in 1987, you don't know who these guys are). Consider this: in 1985, Tommy Herr hit third in the lineup while becoming the last National League player to record over 100 RBIs (110) with fewer than 10 home runs (8). The '85 Orioles had 10 players with more home runs than Herr. In 1987, Herr hit only two home runs and still managed to slap in 83 RBIs. One of those two homers was a walk-off grand slam on seat cushion night. Needless to say, Herr rounded the bases in a torrential downpour of seat cushions.

The Cardinals of the late '90s were the opposite of the teams of the '70s and '80s. Mark McGwire brought the casual fan back to baseball with the long ball. Say what you want, but baseball came back to life in Busch Stadium and Wrigley Field over the late summer of '98. You may think that honoring McGwire's feat is similar to finding yourself humming a Milli Vanilli song, but it existed and it saved baseball. Baseball had a series of strokes beginning in mid-August 1994. Busch Stadium saw the revival of that patient in 1998.

The Cardinals are a national treasure. So let Mark Whiten keep his jersey unbuttoned, let George Hendrick hit with a hat under that helmet, keep Tom Pagnozzi on the roster for years past his prime, and let Mark McGwire lift his 200-pound son over his head at home plate whenever he wants to. Because here's the thing: the Cardinals will always be a Joaquin Andujar tantrum and a David Eckstein single away from a postseason berth.

St. Louis, Missouri / Busch Stadium:
Living five minutes from Chavez Ravine, my daughter thought it was weird that we flew all the way to St. Louis to watch the Dodgers lose to the Cardinals.

SEAN CASEY

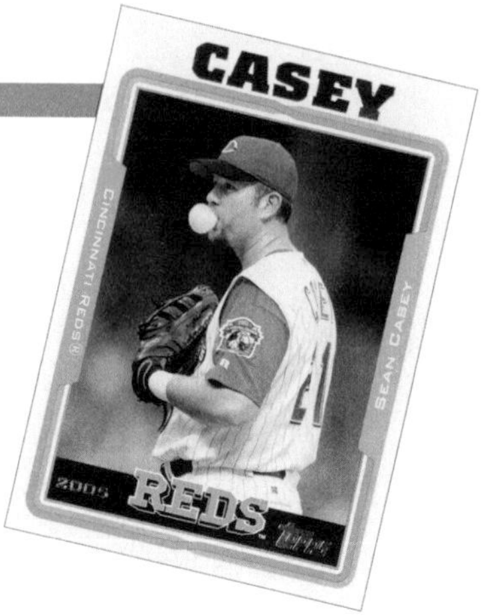
CASEY
CINCINNATI REDS
SEAN CASEY
2005
REDS

ONCE JIM ESSIAN AND RON KARKOVICE RETIRED, CASEY BECAME THE SLOWEST PERSON IN THE MAJOR LEAGUES.

Very few people have been thrown out at first base on a hit to left field. Sean Casey has.

Sean Casey told me that he didn't get one college scholarship offer after hitting for an insanely high average in high school in Pittsburgh. He was fortunate enough to get an invite to play in the Keystone State games in the summer of 1991. He sent out 30 handwritten letters to Division I schools and only the University of Richmond's pitching coach Mark McQueen came. Casey went 4 for 4 with four doubles and eight RBIs. Richmond offered him a $1,000 scholarship. Casey took it and found other ways to pay for the remaining $29,000 a year in tuition. Several years later, Casey was a Cape Cod summer league All-Star ahead of Todd Helton. He still shakes his head in amazement at those two stories, astonished by the improbability of making it to the big leagues. He's a career .302 hitter, so he's probably just being humble.

Known as "the Mayor" because of his friendly demeanor, Casey also was known for his hamstring stretch before entering the batter's box. He told me it was a "little" hamstring stretch, but let's be honest—there was nothing little about it. It was a legitimate, pull-the-car-over-to-the-side-of-the-road-during-a-road-trip-and-get-out-of-the-car stretch.

Casey also did the mule kick at the plate. He would step into the box and bend his left leg so that his left calf touched his left glute. His postswing lumbering to first base on a single was truly something to witness.

WARNING
TRACK
POWER

↑
Just outside the batter's box isn't the best place to get a good stretch in. No matter how loose that hamstring gets, it's still gonna take him a while to get to first base.

↑
Players in major league history: 16,247

Players in major league history who did not do a back-leg mule kick: 16,246

ALL-TIME BEST

PRE-SWING ROUTINE

MIKE HARGROVE

When your nickname is literally "the Human Rain Delay," you're taking too long.

NOMAR GARCIAPARRA

I wonder how long it takes for Nomar to get out of the house in the morning. Getting that front door to close just the right way must be tough.

PABLO SANDOVAL

To anyone who doesn't know or care about baseball: buy a ticket to a San Francisco Giants game and watch Sandoval from the on-deck circle until the first pitch. Unless you hate Bollywood musicals or the prisoners on YouTube dancing to "Thriller," you'll be hooked for life.

JOHNNY DAMON

Royals
18

CERTAIN PEOPLE JUST CAN'T HELP IT. THEY DON'T THINK THEY'RE FLIRTING, BUT THEY ARE. THEY DON'T REALIZE THEY ARE MANIPULATIVE, BUT THEY ARE.

Johnny Damon may be an awesomely humble guy, but everything he does sure makes it seem like he wants to be noticed. For starters, his stance is comically flamboyant. He squats fairly low to the ground and winds his bat around, only to pause like a statue until the pitcher comes to a set position. Then Damon wildly kicks his front leg back, shakes his front heel back and forth, and then swings one-handed, like nobody else in baseball. He hit 24 home runs for the Yankees in 2009, a feat that while I'm sure was helped by the new Yankee Stadium's hitter-friendly environment, is pretty amazing for a guy who seems to swing at the baseball like he's playing tennis.

It really was a shame that Damon had to cut his hair and shave his beard when he signed his fat free-agent contract with the Yankees. The Captain Caveman look that Damon was rocking with the Red Sox was spectacular. Looking like Jason Patric in *Rush* is a great way of standing out and expanding your fan base in a sport that has generally been defined by its very-average-looking players. I'd like to commission a study on Johnny's left arm. Obviously he is talented, fast, clutch, aggressive, and well paid. However, for a guy with so many pluses, his poor arm strength is mystifying. He's had throws cut off by other outfielders. I also don't mean this as an insult, but he really does throw like someone who didn't grow up knowing that baseball existed. There's a 13.5 percent chance that his left arm actually stopped growing when he was 14.

As a batter, his two home runs in game seven of the 2004 ALCS are legendary. He has spent most of the last decade in the playoffs and seems unfazed when the lights are brightest. His nine-pitch at-bat against closer Brad Lidge followed by him stealing second and third base on the same play in game four of the 2009 World Series were remarkable moments of individual effort that rattled an already shaky Lidge, who went on to lose the game for the Phillies. It was the turning point in the Yankees' 27th World Championship.

JOHNNY'S 5-STEP PROGRAM

1

Squat and present the bat to the pitcher

2

Tap your front foot outside of the box

3

High-step leg wiggle

4

Let go of the bat with one hand earlier than anyone else

5

Watch ball leave the yard in meaningful playoff games

MY THOUGHTS ABOUT

THE KANSAS CITY ROYALS and KAUFFMAN STADIUM

I don't wear glasses like Bob Hamelin, my beard never gets as full as Brian McRae's, I've never gotten in a fight with a Weaver brother, and I've never feathered my hair like Jamie Quirk. But I love Kansas City's Kauffman Stadium. I feel a certain respect and awe when I think about Wrigley and Fenway (age, quirkiness, fan ambience). AT&T Park in San Francisco is stunning on a warm, sunny day. Those three are a close second to Kansas City's gem.

What's nuts is that I loved the old Kauffman Stadium before taxpayers spent a bunch of money renovating it. The last time I watched a game in Kansas City they still had really bad AstroTurf covering the field and I sat in the upper deck amid a sparse crowd, watching a Royals team that wasn't very good. Obviously, none of this should add up to something special. But here's the thing: sitting way up high you can see out of the stadium and you get an amazing sense of a stadium's surroundings. And what makes Kansas City so special is that the stadium feels like it's been dropped into the recurring dream I have about playing Little League baseball. It's not a field that's been carved out of an industrial warehouse district or dropped alongside a river or an ocean. It's nestled into a landscape of green, rolling hills. It's a field that feels like where I grew up, in suburban America.

It probably makes no sense that a giant cookie-cutter stadium with little character other than a waterfall could remind me of the Little League field I grew up playing on, but somehow it does. It might be because our Little League games had as many fans as the Royals game I went to, but that's not the full story. I could make a joke about how the Royals hit like my Little League team, but I won't. Sure, the Royals have had a winning record only seven times in the past twenty-four years, but that shouldn't matter. It's about making me feel like a kid again.

I hold out hope that the Royals can make something of themselves in the same way that the Twins, Brewers, and A's have at times competed with the big-market clubs. But it's a tough road. Kansas City isn't a place where players stay. Guys are either on their way up or on their way down when they're on their tour of duty with the Royals. Johnny Damon, Carlos Beltran, and Jermaine Dye played their way out of Kansas City. In my mind, Mike Sweeney, who played 13 seasons with the Royals, did it because he loved how Kauffman Stadium and Kansas City made him feel. He wanted to stay because, as my dad taught me when I used to cry after striking out, it's not just about winning and losing. It's about how it makes you feel.

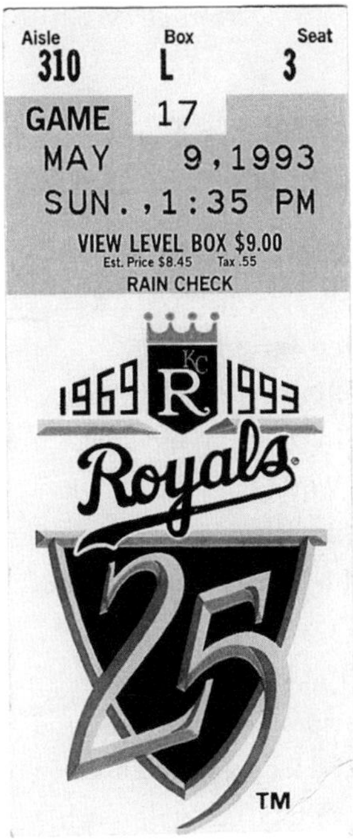
Aisle 310
Box L
Seat 3
GAME 17
MAY 9,1993
SUN.,1:35 PM
VIEW LEVEL BOX $9.00
Est. Price $8.45 Tax .55
RAIN CHECK
1969 KC R 1993
Royals
25
TM

Kansas City, Missouri / Kauffman Stadium (formerly known as Royals Stadium): Nine dollars gets you a rainout in Kansas City.

RON CEY

NL
ALL STAR
3rd Base
RON CEY
DODGERS

RON CEY SHOULD WRITE A BOOK ABOUT HOW TO BE A HOUSEHOLD NAME *WITHOUT* DOING THE FOLLOWING:

1. playing on the Yankees/Red Sox/Mets/Phillies or any other East Coast team;
2. ever finishing in the top 7 in MVP votes;
3. hitting more career home runs than Vinny Castilla, Lance Parrish, or Greg Vaughn;
4. having a career batting average over Rico Brogna's or Ben Grieve's;
5. being involved in a scandal.

It seems impossible, but here's how Cey did it:

1. He played for the Dodgers in four World Series, including three against iconic Yankee teams in the '70s and early '80s.
2. He played out of his mind in the 1981 World Series, both in the field and at the plate, and won the World Series co-MVP.
3. He was the starting third baseman for one of the most beloved NLCS losers of all time, the 1984 Chicago Cubs.
4. He played with first baseman Steve Garvey, second baseman Davey Lopes, and shortstop Bill Russell for eight and a half straight years, a record no one will touch. They were the most enduring infield in baseball history, and it's unlikely a team will ever come close again unless free agency ends and indentured servitude begins, with players required to wear shackles.
5. He had a silly swing, an even sillier running style, and one of the best nicknames ever. Tommy Lasorda nicknamed him "the Penguin" after watching his slow waddle to first base.

Cey's nickname was "the Penguin"

BASEBALL
FEVER

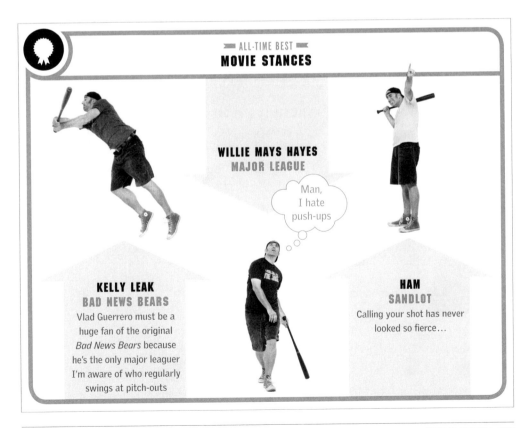

ALL-TIME BEST
MOVIE STANCES

WILLIE MAYS HAYES
MAJOR LEAGUE

Man,
I hate
push-ups

KELLY LEAK
BAD NEWS BEARS

Vlad Guerrero must be a huge fan of the original *Bad News Bears* because he's the only major leaguer I'm aware of who regularly swings at pitch-outs

HAM
SANDLOT

Calling your shot has never looked so fierce…

KIRK GIBSON *vs.* DENNIS ECKERSLEY

CLASSIC MOMENT

WORLD SERIES GAME ONE
OCTOBER 15
1988

1

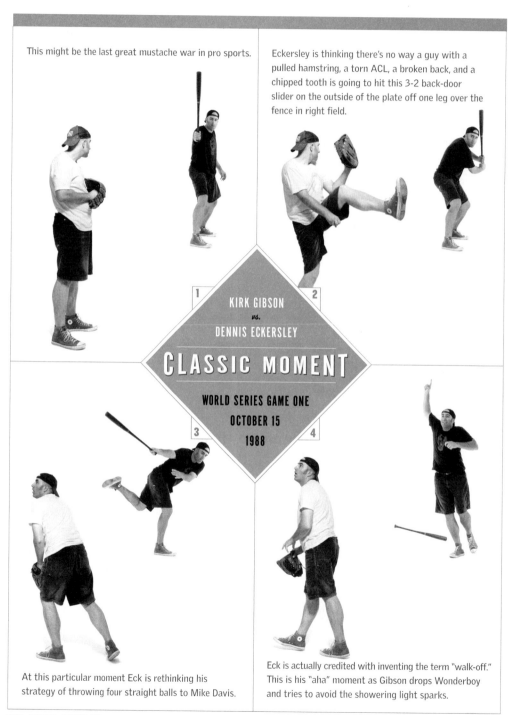

This might be the last great mustache war in pro sports.

2

Eckersley is thinking there's no way a guy with a pulled hamstring, a torn ACL, a broken back, and a chipped tooth is going to hit this 3-2 back-door slider on the outside of the plate off one leg over the fence in right field.

3

At this particular moment Eck is rethinking his strategy of throwing four straight balls to Mike Davis.

4

Eck is actually credited with inventing the term "walk-off." This is his "aha" moment as Gibson drops Wonderboy and tries to avoid the showering light sparks.

MY THOUGHTS ABOUT

THE LOS ANGELES DODGERS *and* DODGER STADIUM

My first major reaction to losing was at the hands of the Dodgers. My family was good friends with former major leaguer Chris Speier and his wife, Aleta. My mom went to high school with Chris, and their son Justin (the major league relief pitcher) and I were born the same year. I grew up in the Bay Area, and Chris played for the Giants for the first six seasons of his major league career, so our families spent time together. Chris was traded to Montreal in 1977 and, out of loyalty to Chris and his family, the Expos became my first true baseball love. Trust me, being a hard-core Expos fan was never a popular or sensible decision, especially in America.

In 1981 the Expos played a day game against the Dodgers in the NLCS. I came home from third grade that afternoon and was greeted by my mom and dad with the news: the Expos had lost 3–1 on a ninth-inning home run by Rick Monday.

What followed were my first real baseball tears. I proceeded to gather up all ten of my mint-condition Rick Monday baseball cards and place them in fireplaces around the neighborhood. I didn't want to burn them alone. I wanted the world (okay, a couple of weirded-out neighbors) to understand my pain. Several years later, my dad turned 40 and went to Dodgertown Fantasy Camp in Vero Beach with his best friend. At the camp he met Rick Monday and told him the story of my tears and subsequent campaign of baseball card terror, to which Monday replied, "You tell him, 'Hi.'" That wasn't quite the response I was hoping for.

I currently live in the shadow of Chavez Ravine. If Los Angeles were New York, I'd walk to Dodger games. But L.A. is L.A. and we love our cars, so I always drive. Whether it's the Lakers or the Dodgers, the knock on L.A. fans is absolutely true: they really do show up late and leave early. In their defense, it's a matter of practicality—traffic in Los Angeles stinks. Running the rush-hour freeway gauntlet and then driving up the hill to Chavez Ravine take time. So don't let the empty seats fool you: Dodger fans are hard-core. Go spend a few innings in the cheap seats and you'll see. They may not have the deep history of the Red Sox or the Yankees, but Dodger fans might be crazier. If tattoos, especially tattoos on the neck or face, are the measure of loyalty to a team, then the Dodgers have a lock on dedication.

It's weird to think that Dodger Stadium is now the third-oldest park in baseball. Built in 1962, it feels like Tomorrowland at Disneyland. It's that era of architecture that now feels retro but not in an old-timey way. It's all smooth concrete and symmetrical arches everywhere. It's a vast and stunningly beautiful park, with a great view of the city. Day games are a bit rough, the sun beating down on you if you're not in the loge section underneath an overhang. Night games are another story. Los Angeles is in the desert, and things cool down at night without actually getting cold. There might not be anything better than sitting up in the cheap seats at Dodger Stadium in July at the end of a Dodger victory and seeing fireworks fill the night sky.

DODGERS.COM
neweracap.com
NEW ERA
DODGERS.COM
NEW ERA
Dodgers
45

Los Angeles, California / Dodger Stadium:
Bazooka gum and sunflower seeds really do taste better in a major league dugout.

BRAD HAWPE

BRAD HAWPE.
ALLEN & GINTER'S
BROOKLYN 2007 NEW YORK

BRAD HAWPE IS A REGAL, ALL-AMERICAN-LOOKING FELLA. Clean-shaven, tall, young, and strapping, he's everything I'm not. When I imitate him I have to take some time to shower and shave. I also have someone stick two live snakes under my clothes. Nervous about the snakes, I kick my hands out toward the strike zone while mule-kicking my knee toward my chest and wiggling my hips to get those snakes off my body and down to my ankles. It's a wonder with all this happening that Hawpe can get a hit, and that he's not screaming like a girl when he's at the plate.

In the pitcher-batter battle, 99 percent of the time the pitcher does more confusing and distracting stuff. He hides the ball behind his leg during his windup, or throws an off-speed pitch, or starts the delivery with a fake grip, or comes from a unique arm angle.

Brad Hawpe is a member of the other 1 percent. When the pitcher and the batter battle, Hawpe wins the war of distraction. The little snake-dance shimmy while the pitcher is throwing has to catch the pitcher off guard. It's why Hawpe won an NCAA championship with LSU in 2000 and is a career .283 hitter who's hit more than 20 home runs in all four of his first full seasons in the National League.

When you become a Colorado Rockie, you're sent a training video in the mail from the management labeled *Stance Madness: This Is Rockies Baseball!* There is an institutional encouragement of high-jinks at the plate in the Rockies organization and the players take it to heart. It's not a coincidence that Don Baylor, once the team's manager, is now the hitting coach. Matt Holliday's knee got higher than his waist before he got traded. Andres Galarraga, tame as an Expo, got to the Rockies and started doing a straight-legged circle lefty leg kick when the pitch was thrown. Yorvit Torrealba, besides having the best name in baseball, does a reverse Joe Morgan at the plate, with his front elbow flapping. Now that he's a Padre, I hope he doesn't lose his stance mojo. Hopefully, hitting coach Randy Ready sees what I see and knows better than to mess with genius.

Busy bat

MY THOUGHTS ABOUT

THE COLORADO ROCKIES *and* MILE HIGH STADIUM / COORS FIELD

In 1993 my buddy Andy McHargue and I drove home to California from college in upstate New York and stopped in Denver to catch a Rockies game. Coors Field was a few years away from being finished, so we went to Mile High Stadium to sit in the Rockpile, a section with $1 seats. One whole dollar. Despite what Sally Struthers tells you, a buck doesn't get you much these days, so it's kind of awesome that you could watch nine innings of Major League Baseball for a dollar. The most hilarious thing about the $1 tickets were the taunts to the crowd in the section right next to us. They'd paid $5 for their seats. Our section taunted them mercilessly for paying five times what we paid for essentially the same seats. I'm going to go out on a limb and say that our section's sense of superiority was misguided.

The Rockies and the Phillies of the '90s looked like beer league softball players. The Blake Street Bombers had mullets for miles, but they were slightly tamer than the '93 Phillies. The Rockies seemed like the band members getting drunk after the show, while the Phils seemed like the band members getting drunk before the show.

Matt Holliday's 2007 season confirmed my suspicion that National League MVP voters don't take Coors Field numbers seriously. Holliday had crazy stats but was second to Jimmy Rollins, whose numbers weren't nearly as gaudy. Ellis Burks, Vinny Castilla, Todd Helton, and Dante Bichette put up silly numbers in Denver. Andres Galarraga and Larry Walker had already put up solid numbers elsewhere, so their home runs are less suspect. Atlanta's Fulton County Stadium was known as the Launching Pad, but Coors Field might as well be the Space Shuttle Launching Pad. The numbers are so wacky that baseballs are placed in a humidor to keep them from drying out in the thin air and becoming easier to hit. Solid career pitchers Darryl Kile, Mike Hampton, and Denny Neagle fell apart in Colorado. Balls just fly out of the park.

Coors Field is the only major league park where I've taken batting practice as an adult. It was an amazing dream to stand at home plate and take pitches. I did my best Troy Tulowitzki imitation and took some big hacks. I can absolutely, unequivocally attest to the thin air in Denver. I hit several of the fat pitches I saw beyond the edge of the infield grass.

Denver, Colorado / Coors Field: When wearing old Chuck Taylors, the top of the dugout is more slippery than you'd think.

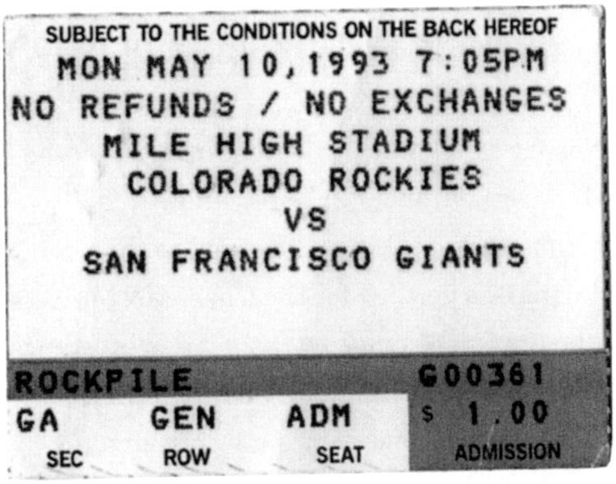

SUBJECT TO THE CONDITIONS ON THE BACK HEREOF
MON MAY 10, 1993 7:05PM
NO REFUNDS / NO EXCHANGES
MILE HIGH STADIUM
COLORADO ROCKIES
VS
SAN FRANCISCO GIANTS

ROCKPILE G00361

GA	GEN	ADM	$ 1.00
SEC	ROW	SEAT	ADMISSION

Mile High Stadium:
This is what a buck got you at Mile High Stadium in 1993.

ALFONSO SORIANO

topps

SORIANO IS IN THIS BOOK BECAUSE HE GIVES ME A WORKOUT.

Nobody gets lower while remaining so closed. He wears number 12. I only know that because he's got his back turned to the pitcher during every at-bat for the Cubs. Most hitters who are low or crouched have an open stance or are at least straight ahead. I think that Soriano is the one stance my chiropractor has a problem with me doing. He's told me repeatedly that you can't bend your legs in a squatting position and then tap one toe and lift one of your legs while keeping your weight evenly distributed. It's just not going to work for your lower back.

Soriano should have gone down in Yankee history as a hero when he hit what should have been the game-winning World Series home run in the 2001 World Series off Curt Schilling in the eighth inning. Unfortunately for him, Tony Womack and Luis Gonzalez ended that dream off Mariano Rivera in the bottom of the ninth.

Soriano also has been sort of miscast in his major league role. Too skinny to be a prolific home-run hitter, he also strikes out too much to be a leadoff hitter. He's a mediocre enough outfielder that it's surprising teams ever put him at second base. He doesn't steal many bases anymore, and his on-base percentage isn't very good. Even with all that, he puts up huge numbers, is a seven-time All-Star and is 10,000% better than me playing "MLB: The Show" against my nephew Zane.

Same finish on:
home run,
strikeout, single,
double,
hit by pitch,
free throw,
putt

1

All Kim can think about is that there's no way this is happening again: two outs in the bottom of the ninth, D-Backs are up two, tying run at the plate, and all he has to do is get one Yankee out. He didn't get it done the night before, but he's not going to make the same mistake twice, right?

2

Kim: Oops. Brosius: snack time.

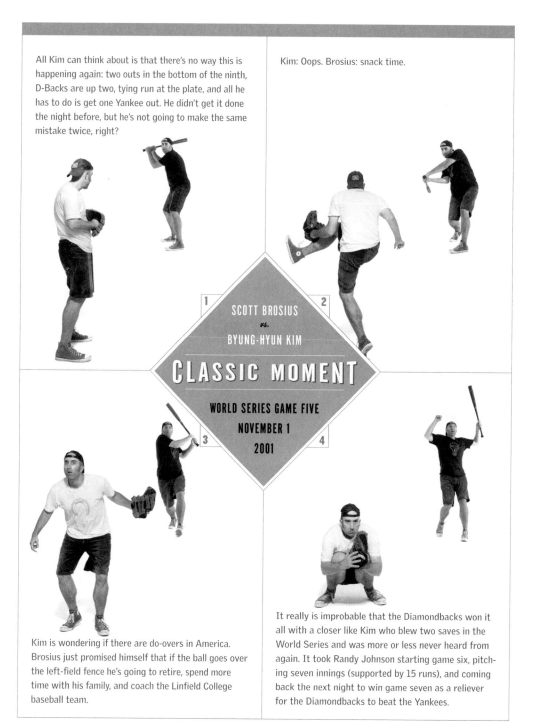

SCOTT BROSIUS

vs.

BYUNG-HYUN KIM

CLASSIC MOMENT

WORLD SERIES GAME FIVE

NOVEMBER 1

2001

3

Kim is wondering if there are do-overs in America. Brosius just promised himself that if the ball goes over the left-field fence he's going to retire, spend more time with his family, and coach the Linfield College baseball team.

4

It really is improbable that the Diamondbacks won it all with a closer like Kim who blew two saves in the World Series and was more or less never heard from again. It took Randy Johnson starting game six, pitching seven innings (supported by 15 runs), and coming back the next night to win game seven as a reliever for the Diamondbacks to beat the Yankees.

MY THOUGHTS ABOUT

THE CHICAGO CUBS *and* WRIGLEY FIELD

I'm not going to say that I feel like a poor man's Forrest Gump, but you might think that when I tell you that I took batting practice at Wrigley Field in 1986. Kids weren't allowed on the field under Manager Jim Frey, but luckily for me he got fired during my weekend trip to Chicago with Justin Speier, son of legendary backup infielder Chris Speier. We woke up early Sunday morning, walked to the stadium, and hit Little League doubles just past the infield grass. It really was surreal, and I was probably a little too young to appreciate how rare an opportunity like that is. What I did take home from that day was the memory of Lee Smith being the biggest human I'd ever stood next to. He really did seem larger than life. It wasn't until I stood next to Manute Bol at the Oakland airport five years later that I had that same feeling.

I based my high school batting stance on Ryne Sandberg's because of one NBC *Game of the Week* that I watched when I was 11. Hall of Famer Bruce Sutter was closing the game for the Cardinals when he gave up a game-tying home run to Sandberg in the bottom of the ninth inning. Incredibly, the Cardinals scored two in the top of the 10th, only to experience Groundhog Day when Sandberg hit another game-tying home run off Sutter in the bottom of the 10th. The Cubs didn't win the game until the 11th inning, but Sandberg's performance was magical. Willie McGee hit for the cycle that day, but trust me, I'm not the only one who has Sandberg's blasts etched into my brain.

Cubs fans probably are the most lovable of all. Unthreatening, kind, and slightly drunk, they're more concerned with the end of beer sales than with whether Alfonso Soriano is going to strike out again. It says a lot that the bleachers are one of the toughest tickets at Wrigley and that some of the most expensive tickets are for the parties on the rooftops of the apartments adjacent to Wrigley on Waveland and Sheffield avenues.

Now that the Curse of the Bambino has been broken for the Red Sox, it sure seems like the Cubs are due for some postseason success. I'm pretty sure Cubs' ownership knows this is true because with the third-highest payroll in baseball, they're spending money like winning should happen. It's funny that more than $130 million gets you four fewer wins than the team with the $30 million payroll. On my list of things I love about baseball, this phenomenon is close to the top. Lou Piniella must look in the mirror in the clubhouse every morning and wonder why he didn't stay semiretired with the Rays in Florida.

My grandpa didn't want to have kids. He was in the navy on a carrier during World War II when a kamikaze pilot made eye contact with him and bombed the carrier with a dud. His ship was given a few weeks of R & R after the bombing and he spent a few nights with his wife, my grandma. Presto, she gets pregnant with my dad. The war ends and he is done with the navy. He gets a job in Southern California but decides to stay in Chicago until my dad is born because "the Cubs were playing well and might make the World Series." They did make the Series that year but lost to the Tigers in seven games. My dad was born on November 5, 1945. The Cubs haven't been back to a World Series since.

Chicago, Illinois / Wrigley Field:
June 29, 1986: taking batting practice on the outfield grass before Dwight Gooden beat Rick Sutcliffe, 7–4, on a Sunday afternoon.

JIM THOME

topps
JIM THOME
INDIANS

MARK DEROSA IS ETCHED IN MY MIND AS THE FIRST TOE-TAPPING BATTER (SORRY, CHIPPER JONES); KENT TEKULVE IS THE FIRST SUBMARINE CLOSER I REMEMBER SEEING (SORRY, DAN QUISENBERRY); AND, IN MY MIND, JIM THOME INVENTED THE SAMURAI POSE.

He is the first true American Ninja. I don't know if Jim's early years in an Illinois dojo influenced him, but I'm pretty sure he can kill a man seven different ways with his bare hands, so you tell me. And he totally would if he wasn't such a nice guy.

What's strange is that Thome doesn't exactly look like a guy who would be influenced by Eastern medicine. That type of guy generally has a ponytail or looks like Billy Zabka in *The Karate Kid*. Thome is a big lug of a man who looks like he'd be working for the city if he wasn't a pro ballplayer. Maybe this is why he really looks like he doesn't know what's happening when he does the samurai pose. He looks sort of befuddled at the plate, like he's clearing cobwebs from his mind as he anticipates the pitch. It's a muted version of B. J. Surhoff's classic expression, which was a my-contact-lens-just-fell-out-and-that's-why-I-look-like-I'm-going-to-cry look.

I've been told two things about Jim Thome.

1. While I was standing on the Metrodome field, a member of the media told me that Thome routinely hits batting-practice homers over the enormous Twins baseball card art murals at the top of the stadium. It is an impossibly far shot. But he hits the ball about that far in games as well. He's hit 500-plus home runs in his career and ranks just behind McGwire, Bonds, Ryan Howard, and Ruth in at-bats per home run. He's also struck out a lot; but who's counting?

2. Various unsolicited comments from ballplayers are that Jim Thome is the nicest player in the league. We aren't even having a conversation about him, and his name surfaces. One player told me that Luis Gonzalez is known as the best tipper in the league, often giving $100 bills to folks opening the door for him. He then went on to say that what's great about Thome is the consistency of how he treats people. He kills people with his kindness, which is pretty awesome because he also could do it with his nunchakus and his throwing stars if he wanted to.

Such an endearing legacy. But is it enough to demand inclusion in this book? Hmmm. Well, I am rooting for him. Carlos Quentin interrupted my thoughts once and barked, "No, you don't understand. He's the nicest man in baseball."

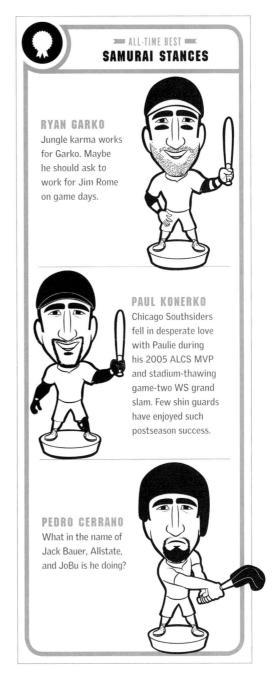

ALL-TIME BEST

SAMURAI STANCES

RYAN GARKO
Jungle karma works for Garko. Maybe he should ask to work for Jim Rome on game days.

PAUL KONERKO
Chicago Southsiders fell in desperate love with Paulie during his 2005 ALCS MVP and stadium-thawing game-two WS grand slam. Few shin guards have enjoyed such postseason success.

PEDRO CERRANO
What in the name of Jack Bauer, Allstate, and JoBu is he doing?

Befuddled look
← detracts from →
menacing bat point
I STILL CALL IT
THE JAKE

MY THOUGHTS ABOUT

THE CLEVELAND INDIANS *and* JACOBS FIELD

One of the many things I love about baseball is the ebb and flow of franchise success. The Indians are a fantastic example of the good and mostly the bad.

Watching the Indians win it all in the movie *Major League* in 1989 was incredibly far-fetched. The Tribe were humorously bad in my youth, and David Ward, the writer and director of that movie, knew exactly what he was doing when he made the Indians' success high comedy.

The Indians lost the 1954 World Series to the New York Giants and didn't make it back to the postseason, let alone the World Series, until 1995. The Red Sox and the Cubs have similar stories, but somehow it seems so much worse in Cleveland. I know Cleveland rocks, but it doesn't rock that hard.

I drove cross-country to and from college a bunch of times with my buddy Andy McHargue. Both big baseball fans, we would stop only in towns with stadiums or interesting sites (the Badlands, Mount Rushmore, the Corn Palace, the largest ball of twine). We would drive through the night to catch ball games before the teams left town. When we arrived at old Municipal Stadium, we got bleacher seats for batting practice. I fell asleep on the left-field bleachers benches because we were 10,000 feet from home plate and nobody was at the game to wake me up. The stadium was amazingly cavernous—74,483 capacity with 73,681 empty seats. The average high school ball field is nicer than Municipal Stadium.

Everything changed in 1994 when Jacobs Field opened. It was truly an "if you build it, they will come" moment. If that field had opened in the late '80s, things would have turned out completely differently for the Indians. First off, it never would have been a "retro" park. It would have been another cavernous, characterless monstrosity. Fan attendance would have continued to be nonexistent, revenue would have been stagnant, and no good players would ever have wanted to play in Cleveland. It's really a *Back to the Future* moment. If Marty's parents don't fall in love on the dance floor, everything disappears.

Jacobs Field and a few Carlos Baergas, Kenny Loftons, Manny Ramirezes, and Mike Hargroves later, the team's fortunes changed. The Indians may be a small-market team that can't keep stars like CC Sabathia and Cliff Lee, but they'll keep making the postseason as long as baseball doesn't get rid of the wild card—that is, unless they change ownership and management and suddenly become the Pirates or the Nationals. Ahhh, the ebb and the flow of a major league franchise. If they ever make *Major League IV: Back on Top*, I'm pretty certain it will center on a ragtag team of goofballs from a down-and-out franchise called the Baltimore Orioles.

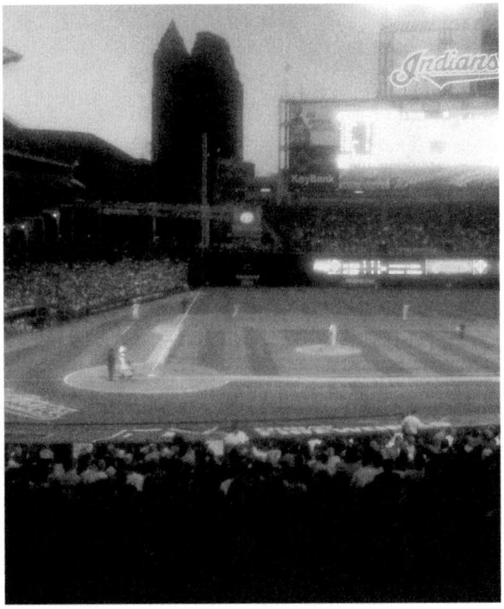
Indians
KeyBank

Cleveland, Ohio / Progressive Field
This game in August 2008 got me temporarily caught up on seeing a game in every current stadium. I'd seen a game in old Municipal Stadium in 1993, and I can tell you that Progressive Field is a huge improvement.

KEN GRIFFEY JR.

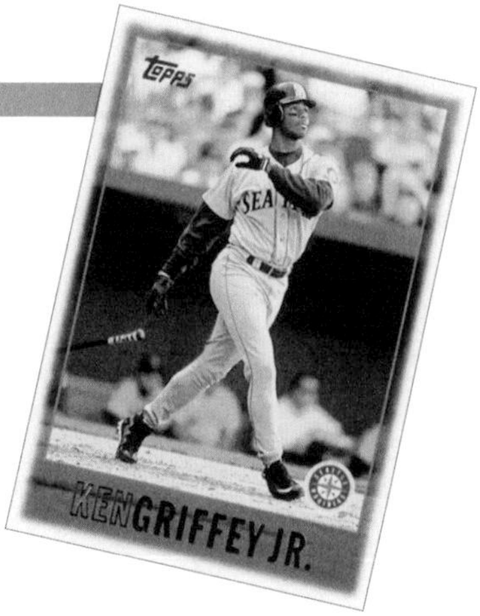
Topps
SEA
KEN GRIFFEY JR.

STAND UPRIGHT, SHIMMYING YOUR SHOULDERS LIKE YOUR THREE-YEAR-OLD DAUGHTER PLAYING PRINCESS, AND REST A LIBRARY ON THE SHELF THAT IS YOUR BOOTY.

Also, when you hit a home run, drop the bat in one fluid motion, act bored and offended that the pitcher dared to throw you that pitch, and begin your pimp walk to first base. Do this and you're Ken Griffey Jr.

Junior is a tricky one for this book because there's a good chance that, as with Joe Morgan and Albert Pujols, his persona and legend trump the actual stance. If Junior has the same stance but is named Mark Merchant or Kevin Reimer or is a career .258 hitter, he isn't mentioned in this book. The kid was blessed with natural talent like we hadn't seen in a long time. He wouldn't stretch before the games or even sweat. So graceful, fluid, and money, the 13-time All-Star and 1997 MVP was born a star. He led the league in home runs four times, yet never bested 56 in a season in an era when players were belting over 60. A 10-time Gold Glover, he made amazing plays in the field, crashing into fences and robbing home runs.

Sadly, all that crashing and robbing led to injuries. Eight of his 21 seasons in the league have been marred by injury. What's insane and slightly sad is that he still hit

630 home runs in those 21 seasons. I really can't imagine what would have happened if he'd stayed healthy and played his whole career with the Mariners. Oh, wait, yes I can. Both Jay Buhner and Edgar Martinez would have a bunch of big, fat World Series rings on their fingers.

The good news for Griffey is that he's the only person to appear as himself on *The Fresh Prince of Bel-Air, Scrubs*, and *The Simpsons*. He's also the only guy in league history to play on the same team as his father. They hit back-to-back home runs off Angel Kirk McCaskill in 1990, which is amazing.

Booty not → to scale

TIM SALMON

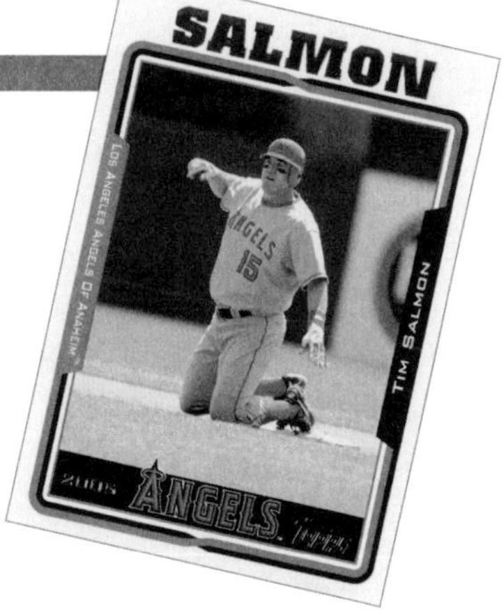
SALMON
LOS ANGELES ANGELS OF ANAHEIM
TIM SALMON
ANGELS
Topps

LIKE LENNY DYKSTRA, TIM SALMON FEATURED TWO DISTINCT STANCES DURING HIS CAREER.

The first one was not interesting, although he did win Rookie of the Year with it and was in the top 7 of the American League MVP voting twice. His late-career stance lands him in this book. Much like Carew, Hrbek, and Yaz, Tim Salmon showed that eventually gravity wins. Kingfish got lower and lower the older he got. In fact, he got so low he became a bulkier Bagwell or a more lumbering Aaron Rowand. Salmon sat in Bagwell's invisible chair while holding the bat directly in front of him and creating a waist-level hoop with his arms that you'd want to throw a basketball through.

Tim Salmon falls into a fantastic category of non–Hall of Famers who spent their entire careers with a single franchise. I'm going to go out on a limb and say that this club isn't going to get bigger anytime soon. Tony Gwynn, Cal Ripken Jr., Robin Yount, and George Brett all played on one team for their careers, but they are Hall of Famers. Besides Salmon, only Kent Hrbek, Jim Gantner, and Bernie Williams come to mind. Jay Buhner played with the Yankees, Ryne Sandberg with the Phillies, and Garret Anderson moved to the Braves, so they're out.

My parents' home phone number has switched area codes three times, which is a lot like looking at Salmon's career stats. He played for the California Angels, the Anaheim Angels, and the Los Angeles Angels of Anaheim (CAL, AA, LAAA). I'm pretty sure if he'd been able to keep playing that he'd be on the Los Angeles California Orange County Angels of America on the Planet in the Universe (LACOCAAPU).

Salmon holds the dubious honor of having the most career home runs in the modern era without an All-Star appearance. Ouch.

But he's still "Mr. Angel" and has a World Series ring to prove it. His performance in the 2002 World Series (.346, 2 home runs, and 5 RBIs including a game-winning homer in game two) will always be remembered by Angels fans, Giants fans, and Felix Rodriguez.

He told me this is
"tapping the nail"

CARL EVERETT

EXPOS
Topps
Expos
Carl EVERETT
OUTFIELD

CARL EVERETT IS TOUGH FOR ME TO FIGURE OUT.

An obvious talent, he was the 10th overall pick in an incredibly deep draft in 1990. It was a draft that featured Chipper Jones and Bret Boone as well as NFL quarterbacks Chris Weinke, Rodney Peete, and Tony Rice. Everett was taken ahead of Troy Percival, Andy Pettitte, Jason Varitek, Garret Anderson, and Jorge Posada. Everett was selected 10 spots ahead of Mike Mussina, who agonizingly gave up a single to Everett after perfectly retiring the first 26 hitters of a 2001 Red Sox/Yankee game.

Everett hit his 200th career home run before Big Papi, Bobby Abreu, Alfonso Soriano, and Nomar Garciaparra. He was a two-time All-Star and key member of the 2005 World Champion White Sox.

All that sounds fantastic, so what makes Carl Everett enigmatic?

Well, he played for eight teams in 14 years. That's an unusually high number of teams saying, Thanks, Carl, but we're not going to need your services next season. Teammates and sportswriters have had field days with his quotes about dinosaurs, lunar landings, and Boston sportswriters being boyfriends. When it comes to crazy, playing a long major league career followed by a minor league stint also puts Everett in odd company that includes Jose Offerman. Yikes.

Everett appeared on my nutso radar in 2000 thanks to umpire Ron Kulpa. During a game, Kulpa had a discussion with Carl about the inner line of the batter's box being compromised by Everett's quirky batting stance. Carl blew his top. I'm sure, based on quotes attributed to Carl, he wasn't trying to kiss Kulpa, but during the ensuing altercation, Everett and Kulpa touched lips, foreheads, and eyeballs as Everett took exception to Kulpa's argument that his stance was illegal. The scene made me think Everett was minutes away from getting his face tattooed, choking basketball coach P. J. Carlesimo, stepping on Cowboys center Andre Gurode's face, clubbing former Dodgers catcher Johnny Roseboro in the head with a bat, threatening to jam a tennis ball down a line judge's throat, and head-butting an Italian soccer player.

I am trying to build a case for the beauty and importance of the quirky batting stance. It's an argument that the stance is art and it's clear that Everett was one passionate artist. Ron Kulpa, please don't burn these books. Let the people have their art.

92% normal
8% not normal

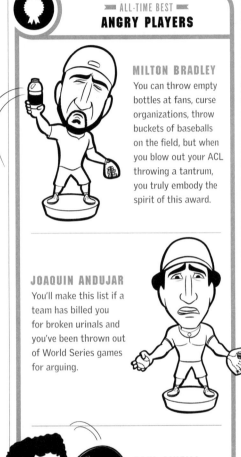

ALL-TIME BEST

ANGRY PLAYERS

MILTON BRADLEY
You can throw empty bottles at fans, curse organizations, throw buckets of baseballs on the field, but when you blow out your ACL throwing a tantrum, you truly embody the spirit of this award.

JOAQUIN ANDUJAR
You'll make this list if a team has billed you for broken urinals and you've been thrown out of World Series games for arguing.

PAUL O'NEILL
Everyone loves this guy, and he gives thoughtful interviews. It reminds me of when neighbors of mass murderers are interviewed on TV and they say, "He seemed so nice."

JASON KENDALL

KENDALL
PITTSBURGH PIRATES®
JASON KENDALL
PIRATES

IT IS AMAZING HOW FEW HOME RUNS JASON KENDALL HAS HIT IN HIS CAREER.

He's a career .290 hitter and yet has hit only 75 home runs in 14 seasons. He's a catcher. Catchers are supposed to strike out a lot and hit for power. He does neither, and I think I know why. He's malnourished. Despite being a three-time All-Star, I don't think he's ever played for a team that paid their players in real money. He spent his first nine years in the league with the Pirates, who paid him in scurvy and plank-walking. Then the A's gave him used copies of *Moneyball* to resell on eBay. And, with the Brewers, let's just assume the beer is free-flowing. Yet, still, not enough spare change to buy batting gloves. Weak with hunger, Kendall didn't have the strength to hit home runs. It's either that or Kendall expended too much energy on his stance to hit for power. Front leg straight, back leg bent, his bare hands waving the bat right in front of his dirty face, with his chaw-filled, pine-tarred head almost in the strike zone. That's a lot going on for one man to handle. We can't all be expected to hit like Sheffield, can we?

Lots of guys in this book have led the league in hit by pitch. That's a curious stat. It's not a flashy stat, but it does get you on base.

And that's what it's all about, isn't it? Kendall is the active career leader, just two spots behind Don Baylor on the all-time list. What does this mean? Do pitchers resent being shown up by hitters? Are there consequences for having flair? Or is it a matter of distraction? Do pitchers get thrown off by all the movement and madness at the plate? Do pitchers get vertigo when they look at a guy like Kendall? Or do Kendall and Baylor just want it more? Is getting on base the only thing they think about and they'll do anything they can to make it happen, including getting plunked?

WARNING-
TRACK
POWER

Butterfly kisses

MY THOUGHTS ABOUT

THE PITTSBURGH PIRATES *and* THREE RIVERS STADIUM / PNC PARK

Do you believe in unconditional love? Not just with your spouses or children or friends but also with your hometown teams? I can't tell you much about Robert Nutting, except that he's the principal owner of the Pittsburgh Pirates and that he must be a big believer in unconditional love. Why else would he give team management the mandate of trading away every single player who holds any significant value? In 2009 the Pirates set a modern-day professional sports franchise record by finishing the season with a losing record for the 17th straight season.

The bad news for fans in Pittsburgh is that there's no end in sight. Since 2003, the Pirates have traded away Jason Bay, Nate McLouth, Freddy Sanchez, Aramis Ramirez, Jason Kendall, Xavier Nady, and Jack Wilson, among others. If they'd kept even a few of these guys, there's a good chance they'd be a halfway decent team. Instead, they lost 99 games in 2009. It's painfully obvious that the Pirates are gaming the revenue sharing system, remaining profitable despite all the losing. Somehow, the team still had 1,577,853 fans attend home games in 2009. That means almost 20,000 people decided it would be fun to go see the Pirates lose on any given day. That really is love.

The Pirates are kind of like my buddy Dan from college, who routinely drafts players who've already been taken during our yearly fantasy football league. Dan, like the Pirates, just doesn't seem to care enough.

My hunch is that Mr. Nutting is a realist. He knows that the Steelers are the kings of Pittsburgh and that fielding a winning baseball team would cost more than the football-centric market would bear.

PNC Park is too good a ballpark for the team it houses. It sends a mixed message that should confuse any true baseball fan. For consistency, the Pirates would be better off playing at old Three Rivers Stadium, a classic, mixed-use hellhole that was blown up in 2001. But PNC Park is certainly one of the main reasons fans attend Pirates games. It's got a phenomenal view of the city, really cheap seats, an intimate feeling, and you can watch all the great former Pirates beat up on the current team.

If I owned the Pirates, here's what I'd do:

1. Rehire Jim Leyland. I'd have to repeal the ban on smoking in the dugout and pay him a bunch of money, but he's a winner, and the Pirates were good when he was steering the ship. Also, seeing him lose his mind after team losses would be hysterical. I can guarantee a spike in postgame press-conference ratings.

2. Bring back the old-school uniforms from the '70s and '80s. It wouldn't be a one-game retro night thing, but a full-season commitment to excellence. Sure, even I know that horizontal striped hats with vertical striped jerseys and pants don't make fashion sense, but they do make a statement. I'd switch back and forth between those silly stripes of the '70s and the mustard yellow they wore in the '80s. Looking like a ripe banana is underrated.

3. Bring Barry Bonds out of retirement. I've heard he still wants to play, and what better way to remind fans of the Pirates' glory years than to bring back a team-first player with credibility and a winning attitude.

I'm not sure any of this would lead to a better team, but at least they'd have flair and style. Go big or go home is what I say.

Pittsburgh, Pennsylvania / PNC Park: Is it me, or does the Pittsburgh skyline look like the inside of the New York, New York casino in Vegas? Beautifully fake.

PIRATES

I'm not sure where a Pirates beach towel ranks on my best stadium giveaways of all time. It's probably a few steps down from the Kevin Costner bobblehead I was handed the night I saw the Inland Empire 66ers play a single-A game in San Bernardino.

BRIAN DOWNING

WHITE SOX
BRIAN DOWNING
CATCHER
SOX

BRIAN DOWNING IS THE BEST EXAMPLE OF A BATTING STANCE ACTUALLY SAVING A CAREER. THAT, AND A COMMITMENT TO HARD WORK, HUSTLE, AND WEIGHT TRAINING.

White Sox fans think of Brian Downing as a middling catcher with a funny haircut and silly glasses. On the first play of his first season in the big leagues with Chicago he wrecked his knee chasing a pop foul, missing most of the season. After five unremarkable seasons with the Sox, Downing got traded to the Angels. In his fifth season with the Angels he started hitting home runs. He opened up his stance as wide as you can for a righty, and knelt low to the ground. When the pitch sailed, he quickly jutted in his left foot to square up his shoulders, only to pop right back open when swinging. He began to crush the ball. He made an All-Star Game, he got MVP votes, he even got contact lenses. With the new stance he spent eight years in the top 10 for hit by pitches.

He was the first player who I heard could bench-press 500 pounds. Who knows if that's true? Who cares? As a kid, it freaked out my brain. I remember they called him "the Incredible Hulk." Looking at the kid who said it, I furrowed my brow, as if to say, "No way. Impossible." Problem is, I had no idea what bench-press meant. Let's just say I had a somewhat sheltered childhood. It was like when my mom declared she couldn't believe Madonna's new album was titled *Like a Virgin*. I remember shaking my head in 11-year-old agreement while thinking, "Uh, what in the world is a virgin?" Oh, I eventually found out the answer, but given my skill set, let's just assume I remained one for a long time.

Downing was "Mr. Angel" before Tim Salmon was "Mr. Angel." It says a lot about a franchise that two of their most beloved players combined for one All-Star Game appearance.

ALL-TIME BEST

GLASSES

TONY GWYNN

Nice-guy Gwynn wearing reflective Oakley Blades made me reevaluate my mistrust of the guys I grew up with who wore Blades, drove Camaros, and hung out at the Gas N' Sip.

CHRIS SABO

Who knew a professional athlete could look like a 51-year-old retired army sergeant who now teaches PE and plays racquetball on the weekends. No offense to people with poor eyesight, but there's no way not to look like a nerd wearing Rec Specs.

DARRELL PORTER

Are there glasses thicker than old Coke bottles? Because if there are, Porter wore them. I'm pretty sure he was legally blind.

Like Tupac, everything changed when Downing went West Coast

MY THOUGHTS ABOUT

THE CHICAGO WHITE SOX *and* COMISKEY PARK / U.S. CELLULAR FIELD

For a team that's been playing in the same city since 1901, I'm not entirely sure why they're not more beloved by the hometown fans. It's a little odd that they play second fiddle to the Cubs even though the Cubs haven't won a World Series since 1908. I can certainly understand why New York fans might favor the Yankees over the Mets. The 27 World Championships of the Yanks certainly trump the two the Mets have won. But the White Sox won the World Series in 2005 and have been pretty competitive in the American League over the past twenty years.

I think it might be because they once wore uniforms with butterfly collars and shorts. It's pretty hard to be taken seriously as a franchise after a stunt like that. The iconic former team owner, Bill Veeck, was famous for doing anything and everything to get fans into the seats, but shorts, Bill? C'mon. Looking like the women's Olympic softball team isn't a great move, especially when you don't have anyone on the team who looks quite like Jennie Finch. I've always appreciated that baseball uniforms left a lot to the imagination. I loved not knowing how absolutely jacked Manny Ramirez was until I saw pictures of him working out during his steroid suspension in tight Under Armor–style gear. I always assumed he had a bit of a gut and chubby legs.

I was at games one and two of the 2005 World Series. It was back when the World Series was still played in October, but it was cold. Watching Scott Podsednik shivering in the on-deck circle in the bottom of the ninth, I never thought in a million years that he'd hit a walk-off home run off closer Brad Lidge. Podsednik didn't hit a single home run in the regular season that year, so I'm sure Lidge was thinking the same thing I was: just don't walk him. This would be reason number 347 for why I don't gamble.

I think that in the fight for the love of a city, the Cubs might win out because of venue. Wrigley Field is cozy and inviting, draped in ivy and nestled in a bustling, residential neighborhood. The stadium is so close to local apartments that fans can watch games from the rooftops of surrounding buildings on Waveland and Sheffield avenues. U.S. Cellular Field, aka Comiskey Park, sits in a desolate strip on the South Side of Chicago, an area that was bulldozed and turned into high-rise public housing in the 1960s. The last of the Robert Taylor Homes, the most notorious of the housing complexes, were demolished in 2007, giving me hope that the area around the ball field might someday not make me feel bad about humanity. The field itself was built right before the retro trend took over, but ownership has done a lot to make the stadium feel less cookie-cutter and soulless.

Chicago, Illinois / U.S. Cellular Field:
Here's me, my dad, and my brother the inning before Konerko hit a grand slam in game two of the World Series in 2005.

I've been to a number of important playoff games and I can confidently say that the crowd reaction to Konerko's homer and Podsednik's walk-off were the most frenzied I've ever seen. Chicago fans absolutely lost their minds.

BASEBALL BEFORE I WAS BORN

I WAS BORN ON OPENING DAY IN 1973.

My first lasting memory of baseball is from 1980. For whatever reason, my obsession with baseball has been focused on players who have played in my lifetime. I haven't spent much time looking at the past. I'm not saying I don't know who Babe Ruth was, but my bear-trap-like mind has mostly closed on players I had a somewhat direct connection with. Many stars of the '70s bled over into the '80s, placing hitters like Joe Morgan, Steve Garvey, Willie Stargell, and Rod Carew on my radar, so I've always felt like I had a pretty broad knowledge of the game and its history.

In mixed company (i.e., when there are old dudes around), I'll get requests for Bobby Tolan, Milt May, Dick McAuliffe, Richie Hebner, Felix Millan, Pete Gray, Ty Cobb, Stan the Man Musial, Willie McCovey, Babe Ruth, Jimmie Foxx, Harmon Killebrew, and Tito Fuentes.

It's perhaps embarrassing to admit that I didn't really know how to imitate these guys until recently. It's perhaps just as shocking to people who know me well that I saw *Bull Durham* for the first time last year. I'm a huge baseball fan, that movie is perhaps the most iconic baseball movie of all time, so me not having every line memorized might sound slightly insane. We all have our blind spots. Anyway, as I've been forced to study some of these older players I've been amazed by their plate high jinks. The art of the stance isn't just a modern creation.

During the summer of 2009 I appeared on the *Late Show* with David Letterman. An hour before taping, the producer ran through a rehearsal where he played the role of Dave. I was told where to walk, where to shake Dave's hand, and where to sit. The producer then sat me down at Dave's desk and asked me questions. He cued me to stand up, grab my bat, and he started to call out players. As I did imitations, I could hear the camera crew laughing, which I took as a good sign. The best sign was a woman's loud laughter coming from a room offstage when I imitated Mark McGwire's bug eyes.

When we were done rehearsing, several crew members started calling out new names. I'm rolling and people are laughing as I fulfill requests for Mickey Rivers, Fred Lynn, and others. The show's director, about my dad's age, barked out an old-school name. "Do Joe Pepitone!" he yelled. I politely told him that I was born in '73 and that I'm not actually 73.

With that said, I will continue to try to build the castle of baseball nostalgia one old-school stance at a time. Because here's the thing: if I keep digging through old-timey players and stats I'll inevitably uncover amazing batting stance artifacts in the ancient ruins of baseball. The statistic that stands out among the

TITO FUENTES

If you're scared of getting hit by a pitch, → this is the stance for you

DICK MCAULIFFE

McAuliffe is the most requested player older than my dad

really old players is the hit-by-pitch category. Stats just don't lie: guys with wacky stances get hit. Two guys from the 1800s, Hughie Jennings and Tommy Tucker, are number 1 and number 3, respectively, on the all-time HBP list and many of the top 100 on the all-time list played at or around the turn of the twentieth century. One of them is named Kid Elberfeld. I mean, c'mon, Kid Elberfeld? He probably got plunked all the time because he dressed like Charlie Chaplin and threw pies at the pitcher. Throw in the newness of the game and the presumable lack of formal training and coaching and I have to believe everyone in the league was a Kid Elberfeld. Technology, scouting, and early training have led to a watered-down world of stance. Kid Elberfeld was probably raised by wolves and made the majors because a scout saw him swing a mallet at a carnival and figured he'd be able to hit the ball a long way. Raw and undisciplined, Kid Elberfeld probably tried to eat the ball the first time someone threw it his way. He wasn't a caveman, but he probably wasn't far off compared to the polished professional children of today's game who learn how to swing like J. D. Drew and throw like Jeter. I'm just saying.

WILLIE MCCOVEY

I did a report on McCovey when I was in second grade and it should be obvious why ↓

FELIX MILLAN

"Choking up" should be called "Millaning" ↓

STAN MUSIAL

← Musial's statue outside Busch Stadium is the greatest bronzed stance of all time

BOBBY TOLAN

If you're a below-average journeyman and you want people to remember → you 40 years from now, do something wacky at the plate. Just ask Bobby Tolan

ROY WHITE

White and his stance → lived in the World Series in the '70s. Apparently, hiding the bat from the pitcher worked for him

NO MAS

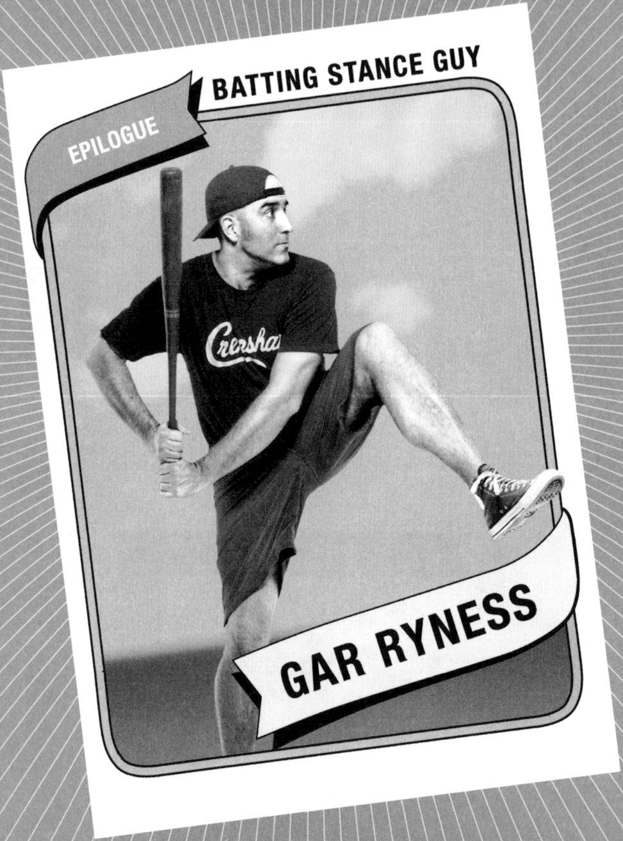
BATTING STANCE GUY
EPILOGUE
GAR RYNESS

MY WALK-OFF

AS I'VE CLEARLY PROVEN, I'M NO BASEBALL EXPERT.

I'm not a historian and I'm not a number-cruncher. I'm just a fan. With that said, I've noticed a few things about batting stances that are probably worth highlighting.

First, a crazy stance will get you hit. Hit by pitches, that is. There are more than 16,000 players in major league baseball history. Of the 50 players featured in this book, 41 of them are in the top 912 all-time HBP category. Of those 41, 31 are in the top 500, 15 are in the top 200, and 2 are in the top 5 of all time (Don Baylor and Jason Kendall). I'm not a mathematician but I've read several chapters of *Freakonomics*, so I know that numbers like this don't lie.

What I can't tell you is why goofiness at the plate gets you plunked. Do pitchers get distracted by the hitter's antics? Do pitchers resent the showmanship of the more flamboyant hitters and hit them to send a message? Do antics at the plate also mean you crowd the plate? Or, do plate high jinks mean you're just really good so you'll always have a target on your back or shoulder or leg or head? I'm not sure anyone will ever have the answer. Just know that if your dream is to become the next Pete Rose (tied for 57th on the all-time HBP list), you better be psychologically ready to step into the box and do something unusual.

But what about the idea that a crazy stance makes you better? Possibly. The 50 players in this book finished their careers in the top 5 percent of all major leaguers in offensive totals. I guess it shouldn't be surprising that nine of my Top 50 were in the 1979 All-Star Game (Rose, Morgan, Matthews, Downing, Carew, Baylor, Kingman, Jack Clark, and Ron Cey) and eight were in the 1998 All-Star Game (Ripken, Sheffield, Alou, Boone, Vaughn, Thome, Griffey, and Kendall). In all, the Top 50 combined for 189 All-Star appearances. Now, I know what you're thinking: I remember all these guys and their stances because they were All-Stars to begin with. If a stance happens in the woods, or let's say on the 2006 Pirates, would anyone care? You might be a little right, but trust me when I say that I remember stances, not stars. I'm not sure how many times I saw Tony Eusebio play, but his stance is more firmly stuck in my brain than his 30 career home runs would suggest.

% THIS BOOK IN NUMBERS

In numerical terms, a composite of the 50 hitters in this book looks like this kind of hitter:

15-YEAR
MLB career

.279 CAREER AVERAGE
Andre Dawson, all-time rank #612

1,745 HITS
Kent Hrbek #384

228 HOME RUNS
Howard Johnson #234

889 RBIs
Richie Hebner #344

983 RUNS
Sal Bando #324

314 DOUBLES
Bert Campaneris #350

37 TRIPLES
Darryl Strawberry #977—okay, clearly not the fastest bunch

174 STOLEN BASES
Mike Schmidt #415

778 BASE ON BALLS
Joe Torre #258

Those are pretty solid numbers. It has me thinking that Little League coaches misguide their youth. Most of us had a coach who told us to quit screwing around and bend your knees and hit right. That there is a correct way to stand at the plate. That you need to hold your hands here, don't wiggle too much, stay still, stride a little with this foot, don't step in the bucket, cut your hair, get a job. All that sounds like nothing any of the players in this book ever did with any consistency.

What coaches should be saying, and what professional players do say when you ask them about their stance, is that it's about what makes you comfortable at the plate.

Here's what the success of the hitters in this book really shows: If you're good and you produce, you can do whatever you want at the plate to make yourself comfortable. It's just a little sad that you're not allowed to enjoy yourself before you've made it to the big leagues.

Shouldn't we look at major league players for all that they are at the plate and realize that individuality and fun and jazz hands and magic are okay? It's still just a game, right? A dream of A-Rod's contract and Jeter's sponsorships isn't what motivates kids, is it? As kids we imitate our baseball heroes at the plate because it's fantasy and because it's fun to pretend. We picture ourselves in that clutch moment, with the game on the line, with everything at stake and the crowd going wild. Can someone explain to me why that has to end when the game is real?

The problem with baseball (and I say this out of love) is how serious the game has become. From Little League to the minors to the pros, baseball is a machine of tradition and intensity. For a game that doesn't have the violence of football or the physicality of basketball, it's weird to me that the hilarity and quirkiness and eccentricity of the game, its traditions, and its players aren't more celebrated.

I think we can have our baseball cake and eat it, too. Why can't it be everything it is now, and has been, but a whole lot more fun? I'm not suggesting changing anything, exactly. I'm not advocating speeding up the game or adding more instant replay. I'm just asking that if you're a fan, young or old, or an amateur or a professional, that you really take a look at the things that make the game great and adjust your vision. Remind yourself with a slap to your head or a nudge to your ribs that it's funny. Even in the most intense of moments, with the bases loaded and two outs in the bottom of the ninth with your team down three runs, what your favorite hitter is doing at the plate is downright hilarious.

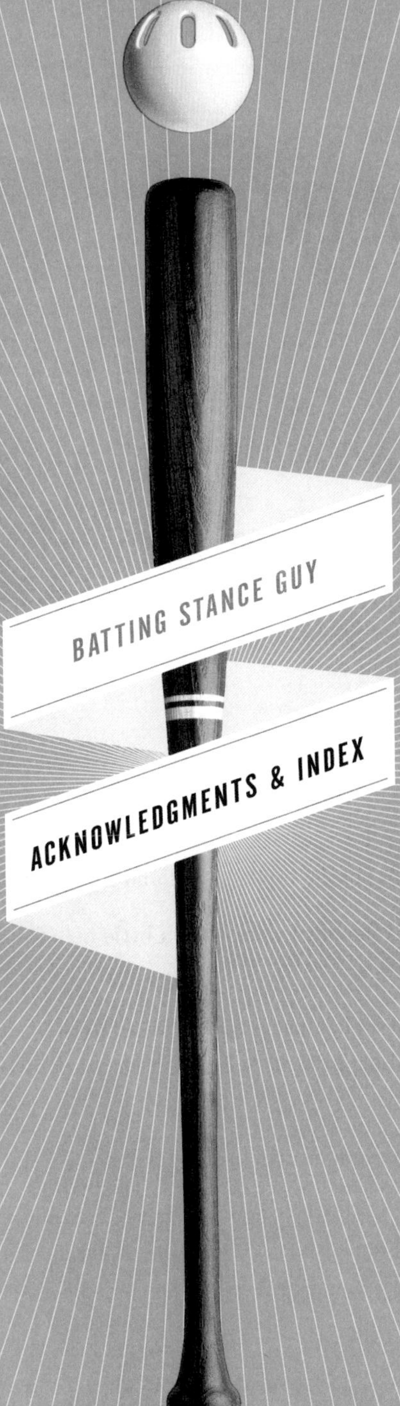

BATTING STANCE GUY

ACKNOWLEDGMENTS & INDEX

ACKNOWLEDGMENTS

We'd like to thank the following:

Ryan Long for being the third head of the BSG monster.

Peter Eliasberg for lending his time and voice to many a backyard video. If he wasn't too busy arguing cases before the Supreme Court he might have been able to help us write a better book.

Natalie Long for her bobblehead genius.

Baldwin Smith, Clinton Pickens, Matt Ricatto, and Chris Hannan for being early supporters and believers.

Farley Chase and Brant Rumble for loving baseball and making this book happen.

Brian Chojnowski for doing all the hard work with a little help from his favorite uncle, Bill Ross.

No Mas for all the shirts for the book, especially the "Rated Rookie" shirt that makes Gar feel like Steve Jeltz and Todd Zeile. To get the shirts worn by Gar in this book go to nomas-nyc.com.

Dimitri Newman for his photographic expertise.

The really smart people at baseball-reference.com. Every real statistic in this book was either confirmed or discovered at baseball-reference.com. If any statistics in the book are incorrect, it's either because we made them up for comedic effect or misread them on baseball-reference.com

To Topps and The Wiffle Ball, Inc., for lending their images to the book.

Michael Hermann at Wicked Cow Entertainment.

Gar would also like to thank Jon Pyle, Jason Sorge, Nate Daniels, SUFFL, Dr Z, Joby Harris, Alison Treleaven, Cobra Kai, Rob Bradford, Mike Konner and, why not, all of Day 8, Eric Burak, Erich Manwarren, David Letterman, Bill Simmons, Dan Patrick, Greg Hanlon, Kent Krosbakken, Benjamin Hochman, Martin Khodabashian, Jonathan Mills, Hetschel's, Spud Sanders, Naoto Ishikawa, Rick Ambrozic, Harold Reynolds, Christopher Isenberg, Alan Schutz, Kevin Gugle, Appleton Gang, everybody associated with the film *The Natural*, GBNB, Mom & Dad. Thank you to anyone who indulged, listened, or shouted out stances, even you Aunt Barbara. Lisa, for letting me borrow Caleb for two years. Caleb, this thing doesn't happen without you.

And mostly, Rebecca, lovely enough to believe in me, sacrificial enough to just smile and nod while I talk baseball.

Caleb would also like to thank his parents, Mary and Mac, and most important, his wife, Lisa, for being loving, patient, and supportive. He should also probably thank Gar because the last two years wouldn't have happened if it wasn't for him.

INDEX

GUYS WHO GET MENTIONED AN EMBARRASSING NUMBER OF TIMES

HITTERS NOT IN TOP 50

PITCHERS

BUDDIES

MANAGERS/COACHES

FOOTBALL PLAYERS

BASKETBALL PLAYERS

POP CULTURE

MUSICAL REFERENCES INCLUDED FOR NO PARTICULAR REASON

GUYS WHO WEAR SUITS

WOMEN WHO MIGHT BE SURPRISED THAT THEY'RE IN A BOOK ABOUT BATTING STANCES

FAN INTERFERENCE

GUESS THE STANCE

There are hundreds of deserving hitters who didn't make the Top 50, enough to fill a book or two or three. In their honor, here's a five-stance quiz to test your stance IQ. There isn't an answer key so don't bother looking, although you can go to www.battingstanceguy.com to find out more.

Hint: This is a home run off Doc Ellis in the 1971 All-Star Game.

Hint: *Normal Stance* (2005–2008) = No All-Star appearances, no Gold Glove, no Silver Slugger.

Wacky Stance (2009) = All-Star, Gold Glove, Silver Slugger, and a 30-game hitting streak.

Hint: This may be my favorite stance and swing of all time and while it's the one I use in slow-pitch softball to go opposite field, it doesn't crack the Top 50 because it was just too smooth.

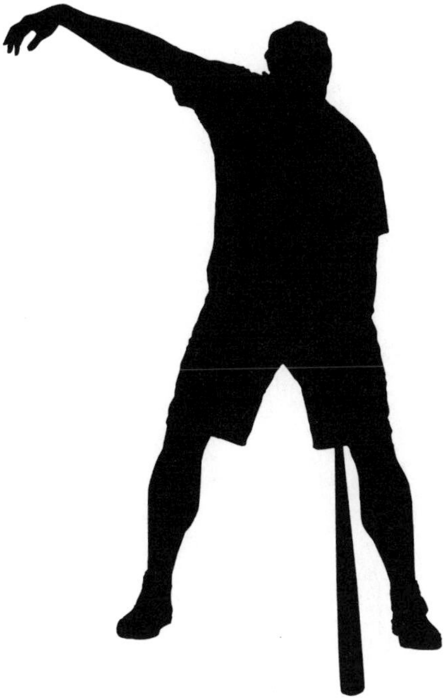

Hint: If you don't know who this is then you haven't been watching the last 14 years of postseason baseball.

Hint: I wonder if his manager will get in trouble for tweeting about this player's one-handed post-hit bat flings.